LATE BLOOMERS

LATE BLOOMERS

AWAKENING TO LESBIANISM AFTER FORTY

Robin McCoy

Writers Club Press

San Jose New York Lincoln Shanghai

late bloomers
Awakening to Lesbianism After Forty

Writers Club Press
an imprint of iUniverse.com, Inc.

For information address:
iUniverse.com, Inc.
5220 S 16th, Ste. 200
Lincoln, NE 68512
www.iuniverse.com

ISBN: 0-595-16227-4

Printed in the United States of America

To the Late Bloomers who enriched my own life.
Deepest thanks for the leaps you took.

Contents

Acknowledgments

I extend my sincere appreciation to all those women who contributed to this work. It could not have been written without the generous survey respondents and the courageous, talented submissions of personal anecdotes, histories, and stories.

Introduction

These are the stories of women I call "late bloomers," women who lived forty or more years as heterosexuals, unaware of or unwilling to acknowledge a latent lesbianism. In these pages you will meet many unique women, all celebrating a common experience as they tell their sexy, funny, joyful, and sometimes painful tales of self-discovery.

I began this project with questions that had been nagging me for some time. What are the causes and what are the repercussions of a mid-life conversion to homosexuality? What could trigger such a transformation? Was this a question of suppressing one's true nature or a gradual remaking of one's nature?

My interest was partly personal, as I have two friends to whom this has happened. One was forty-two, the other fifty-two, when they embarked on their first lesbian relationship. Both of them claimed never to have considered women as potential lovers before it happened to them, and both have remained with women since.

It seems extraordinary, at least to me, that intelligent, introspective women like my two friends could have such an identity-changing experience after forty. Is this one possible manifestation of the purported mid-life crisis? I wondered. Is this what normal, red-blooded American females have to look forward to—hot flashes and sex with Judy? Talk about "the change"!

Most people like to think that they know themselves pretty well by middle-age. But forty has traditionally been a tricky age for women. It signals the end of youth and the slide towards the end of fertility. It signals the beginning of a new phase, not coincidentally the time when the kids leave home. In their forties, women often reexamine their goals and desires. They also often invest more energy into careers and activities outside the home. They begin to venture into new arenas and find things out about the identity they ignored for most of their lives. Or maybe their identity just changes. We are evolving, all of us, all of the time. There's no reason to think ourselves incapable of surprises after forty. Perhaps it is that self-assurance that makes us vulnerable.

This book is an attempt to examine the transformation from straight to gay, the "blooming" phase, and perhaps answer some of my original questions. In researching this subject, I collected questionnaire results and personal stories from 100 women, women from across the country who possess a wide range of experiences. There is nothing scientific about these results. The contributors represent a small minority of a larger minority of our population, and just happen to be the women who responded. Though unscientific, the statistics are interesting.

In age, they range from forty to sixty-four. Seventy-five percent are educated professionals, and the best represented careers are health care (41%) and teaching (16%). Most of these women are divorced (65%) and many of those ended marriages of twenty years or more (35%). One woman is still married, and thirty-four percent have never been married. Four percent of respondents have never had sex with a man, while twenty percent have never had sex with a woman. This last group is represented in the final chapter.

These women may belong to the last generation for whom homosexuality wasn't an option, maybe wasn't even a thought. They grew up in the fifties or earlier, the decade of the dutiful homemaker, when, as one woman put it, "homosexuals were rarely mentioned, but when they were, they were odd and pathetic men, and there were none in our state."

"I remember looking up the word 'lesbian' in a dictionary," writes one woman, "and after reading the definition, still didn't know anything. I did eventually locate Lesbos on a globe, that being the island they came from. Of course there was no one you could ask."

Without the option of lesbianism, and given the prevailing attitude towards career women, the default for most women of the day was marriage and children. Thirty percent of my respondents were married young (by early twenties) and raised families.

For young women now, lesbianism is an option, though still not an easy one. They can hardly help hearing about it, and it's much more likely that lesbians they know will be "out," so the subject can be discussed. Another difference for young women now is that they take for granted that they won't have to have a husband to support them. Financial freedom opens up the door for all sorts of other freedoms, including the freedom to love whomever one chooses. And these days, practically every sitcom on television has gay characters; we are very much represented in our popular culture. All but the most right-wing politicos would not dare to disparage homosexuality as a lifestyle in public. Things have certainly changed since I was a youngster.

For most gays and lesbians, their sexual identity made itself known from an early age, often in preadolescent childhood. This is one of the factors used to support the view that homosexuality is not a choice. Sixty-eight percent of the women in the survey recognize childhood or adolescent signs that they were lesbians, usually sexual or at least doting attraction to females. But they managed to deny and suppress these early signs until middle age. Eighty percent of my respondents believe that their lesbianism is innate or genetically determined.

If so, why were they able to lead a heterosexual life into middle age with, in many cases, no clue that something was amiss? Forty-four percent said that they believed their early heterosexual life was an attempt at self delusion. Eighty-four percent do not believe that they could ever be happy in a heterosexual relationship in the future.

I was especially interested in the "trigger" for these women, the thing that caused them, after a lifetime of denial in many cases, to recognize their attraction to women. As it turned out, the most common trigger was becoming friends with a lesbian. Thinking about lesbianism piqued an interest, and an interest led to action. One woman said that she couldn't stop fantasizing about what her friend and her lover did in bed. The fantasies were graphic and intense, and before long, she had placed herself in them.

The trigger itself could be almost anything—a movie, a Caesar salad, a Georgia O' Keefe painting. For most women, the process was gradual, an awakening transgressing through several stages of awareness. If nothing had triggered the transformation for these women, they might have continued to be happy, healthy members of the majority. Except that even if they didn't know it consciously, on some level, they did know. That seems obvious in how easily most of them made the switch. Also, a full ninety-eight percent of respondents said that they were happier now, after acknowledging their lesbianism, whether or not they have had a female lover. The other two percent didn't say they weren't happier; they just didn't answer the question because "happier" wasn't the way they wanted to describe themselves.

The stories of heterosexual life contain a constant theme of restlessness and dissatisfaction. There are marriages without intimacy, unfulfilling promiscuity, and long periods of self-enforced celibacy resulting from unsatisfactory relationships with men.

An overriding emotion associated with finally realizing love for women was joy. Over and over again the words used to describe these new relationships are "natural," "equal," and "intimate." And, of course, "passionate." Some of these forty-something women had never before enjoyed sex. Ultimately, these are stories of self discovery, not just of a sexual identity, but of a much larger personal one. (Being a lesbian isn't just about having sex with women, after all.) Self discovery sometimes happens suddenly, in a epiphany of realization. Sometimes it takes a lifetime. For many of these women, it took at least forty years.

Those who participated in the survey generally felt gratitude, hope, and a sense of freedom as a result of their new sexual identity. Only ten percent said they had sought professional counseling related to their lesbianism. As one woman said, "I think things happen when you're able to cope with them. There may be a lot of truth in that. For women of earlier generations, the time may never have come. For the women now in their forties, fifties, and sixties, the time may be now. For women of my generation, those on the cusp of forty, the sexual awareness of the sixties and seventies made it easier to grow up feeling comfortable about alternative lifestyles. And for the younger generation, the alternatives are more prominent than ever. It may well be that there will be far fewer late bloomers in the future. In fact, there is something of a movement among young women to cash in on what they see as the "lesbian chic" of the day. Who would have thought it back at Stonewall?

This is not to say that adopting a lesbian lifestyle today is a simple, painless transition. Obviously, some of these women struggled with it for decades. Some of them are still struggling. And we are reminded far too often about the taunting and physical abuse gay people suffer from those who are trying to force us back into the closet. But for the most part, so much progress has been made in recent years that it is hard to imagine the stories contained in this volume being written in the future.

Having "come home" at last, most of these women are understandably anxious to make up for lost time. In general, many homosexuals resent the difficult years they spend trying to be straight, dating the opposite sex and struggling with their sexuality. They feel they missed something in the early years. I expected some of the over-40 respondents to feel the same way, more strongly even because of the additional time they had lived a heterosexual lifestyle. And some of them did. Some of them regretted the long, unhappy "lie" that was their early life. But some of them felt quite differently. One woman said that she felt "blessed to have known so many facets of myself."

If the early heterosexual experiences were especially unhappy, the convert was generally more bitter about the past. In one case, a woman told me that she was in an unhappy marriage with a now very old man, had been married almost thirty years, knew she was a lesbian, but had never so much as kissed a woman. She had told no one about her sexual identity. Her letter was full of anguish, and I wept reading it. One woman, once she realized that she was a lesbian, wrote to all her friends and told them so. When several responded that they already knew, she felt discouraged, thinking, "Why didn't they tell me?" In most cases, however, there was a spirit of celebration among these women. Their sense of gratitude for whatever or whomever awakened them was huge. They were thankful to have made the discovery, even though it came during middle age. Even when their first lesbian affair was tragic, even when their first lesbian lover treated them basely, they were still grateful. One woman said, typically, "if a man had done that to me, I'd have singed the hair off his balls with a blowtorch." But of the woman who "had done that" to her, she says she will always love her. There's no bitterness or regret. This attitude results, of course, from having waited so long.

The stories that follow are grouped based on how the transformation came about, each section containing typical accounts from among those provided by survey participants. Preceding each section are quotations from the many letters and stories I received. I have edited the stories where appropriate, and have in every case used fictional names.

I wish to thank everyone who responded for your generous contributions. These are your stories, these are your lives, and this is my way of saluting the thousands of beautiful blooms sprouting across the country. Could the phrase "better late than never" ever be more aptly applied?

1

I've Been Vamped

She was a student, a good student, but she didn't learn this from me.

I couldn't really say she forced herself on me. After all, I was the one who booked us a room with a single king-sized bed.

It happened so fast, I still can't recall the details. She knew exactly what buttons to push.

*　　　　　*　　　　　*

These are the stories of women who were aggressively seduced by a lesbian. Prior to the seduction, they had no acknowledged inclination towards homosexuality. After, however, they were converts.

The implication that comes through in these stories is that the lesbian wouldn't have been attracted in the first place if there wasn't some suggestion that the seductee was ready and willing. Even if the conscious doesn't acknowledge the desire for women, the subconscious may be putting out signals (isn't this how gaydar works?). Women who are tuned in to those signals may then be drawn in.

Most of these women recognized later that they hadn't been simply innocent bystanders on the lesbian rampage path. One woman admitted that without even being aware of her behavior, she had taken to going braless and wearing revealing blouses when she and her lesbian friend were together. More often, the subconscious come-on was verbal, sex talk being a popular factor. Sometimes, though, the seductee was a thoroughly passive participant, at least prior to the actual seduction. She didn't bat her eyes or wear aviator goggles (that is a universal turn-on, isn't it?) or do anything to entice the other woman.

These are the women who, after their first lesbian experience, are left sort of confused, wondering if they're lesbians or not. They found the experience exotic, refreshing, exhilarating even, and now they're asking themselves, "What was that?" Imagine the look on the coyote's face just after the roadrunner blitzes by leaving a stick of dynamite in each of his ears.

For the women in this section, most first relationships were short-lived and sexually explosive, but have had long-term impact. Being seduced by another woman, a frightening experience for the majority of these women, has been a powerful blow to their entrenched beliefs. In these cases, however, it has left them longing for more of the same.

June's Story

It was the way she looked at me as she asked, her tone of voice, that made me suspect she was interested in more than my opinion of M. F. K. Fisher.

I'd known Julie for years, not well, but enough to have a conversation about a book or a writer. I was a librarian and she was a reader, a studious young woman. By the time we got together for what would be a major turning point in my life, she was working on a master's degree.

Before Julie, I was fiercely heterosexual, and, I admit, promiscuous. There were one-night stands, summer flings, hot-tub quickies. The one long-term relationship I had was with a man who lived in another state who came to visit a couple of times a year.

I'd always thought that the reason I hadn't married or "settled down" was that I just hadn't met the right man. Later, I realized that there was no right man for me. Julie, twenty-four and a lesbian searching for her first female lover, latched onto what she considered secret messages from me to her. I was reading May Sarton, lesbian novelist. I read Susan Griffin, lesbian poet. I was gushingly admiring of strong, independent women.

Looking back, I can see why she thought I was a lesbian. I once flew from New Mexico to the East Coast to visit May Sarton for a few minutes and tell her how much I admired her work. I told this story to Julie. What was she to think?

One evening, as I helped her with her research, she asked, "Can we go to dinner some time?"

I remember feeling a mixture of fear and excitement. Was this a date, I wondered. It was the way she looked at me as she asked, her tone of voice, that made me suspect she was interested in more than my opinion of M. F. K. Fisher.

"Sure," I said, with mock nonchalance.

I was already curious, obviously, about women who loved women. I was curious, but didn't think I was one. I'd never been attracted to women, physically. And one could point to that long trail of spent penises to prove how much I enjoyed men.

We went to dinner, a meal of tacos and refried beans that lasted until the restaurant closed. It seemed we couldn't stop talking to one another. It was exhausting, that evening.

When she dropped me off at my house, she said good night with an awkward squeeze of my shoulder that left me certain of her interest. It was here that the alarm should have gone off, that a heterosexual woman would have said to herself, "Don't let this go any further." So what did this heterosexual woman do? I invited her to dinner at my house.

One thing I really admired about Julie was her honesty. The night she came for dinner, she told me straight out that she was a lesbian and that she was interested in me. She told me about her heartbreaking love for a straight woman who couldn't reciprocate. Julie had never made love to a woman, but had always known she was a lesbian. "I'm not interested in a non-physical friendship with you," she said. "If you're sure you don't want what I want, tell me now. If you're not sure, I can be patient and we'll just see how things go."

Basically what she was saying was that she didn't want to waste her time on me if there was no chance. So if I said I wasn't interested, which is what I thought, I wouldn't see her again. What could I say? I said I wasn't sure. Okay, she said, and we talked about other things. It was a long evening. I liked her. She was intelligent and quick-witted. She was full of humor, the sort of cynical wry humor I admired in others, but could never carry off myself.

Eventually she prepared to leave. Just inside the door, she asked, "Can I kiss you goodnight?" Thrown off, I said, "Uh, how about a hug instead?" I'd never kissed a woman and didn't want to. The idea was scary and it didn't seem right.

She shrugged her shoulders and moved closer. I put my arms around her in a tight, reassuring embrace. I don't think she intended this as a trap, but when I moved to leave her arms, she held me and didn't seem inclined to relax her grip. Our bodies were pressed against each other, her hands were on my back. I heard her breathe deeply, her head on my shoulder.

What do I do now, I thought. I wasn't afraid, just uncertain. I didn't want to hurt her feelings. I knew how badly she yearned for the touch of a woman. While I was debating with myself, Julie touched her lips to my neck, tentatively and gently. I could tell by the way she breathed that she was highly aroused by this closeness. When she looked into my eyes, I could see the lust pouring out. She moved to kiss my mouth, and I turned my head. She kissed my cheek, so tenderly, inconsistent with her blatant desire.

We held each other, there inside the door, her lips on my face and neck, softly grazing the skin. She held me tightly against her, kissing with her lips and tongue. "You feel so good," she said, her hot breath in my ear. By now it was feeling pretty good to me too. Julie sucked my ear lobe, ran her tongue around the curves of my ear, breathing into the wetness.

When she kissed my collar bone, I thought I'd go into orbit. She was so gentle, but the energy and the passion moving between our bodies was intense and surging. I felt her lips teasing the corner of my mouth. She desperately wanted to kiss my mouth.

She's not going to let me go, I thought, until she wins this battle. What the hell, I decided, turning slightly so that our lips met.

I've never been kissed like that before. It was indescribable. Our mouths seemed to belong to one another. Spasm after spasm of desire swept through me. I couldn't believe how wonderful it was to kiss her. We must have stood there for at least an hour until at last Julie pulled herself away. She smiled affectionately and touched my cheek "Thank you," she said.

With one final lingering kiss, she was gone. I stood transfixed, my underwear and shorts soaked through, afraid to even think. I invited her to dinner again the following week. My anticipation was so great that I couldn't stop trembling. I wanted her, I knew that. I wanted her to touch me. I fantasized all week about making love with her.

And I was so grateful that she had pushed me because I'd needed to be pushed. I was forty-two years old. If not for Julie, how long would it have been?

We made love that night, all night, and both of us had orgasm after orgasm. They came in waves. I felt a kind of sexual satisfaction I'd never known was possible, exhaustion really. We couldn't stop loving each other. When we awoke in the morning we made love again. As she was saying goodbye in the living room, we kissed and ended up on the floor in another passionate interlude. There was no end to this passion. I was amazed at my capacity for lust.

My affair with Julie was the most intense physical experience I've ever had. Although we are no longer together, I'll always love her and I'll always thank God that she came into my life and opened my eyes and my heart to loving women. She'd been able to see what was lurking in me. As she told me, she'd been convinced when she asked me out that I was a lesbian. It was written all over me, she said, and she'd been very surprised when I told her I wasn't, that evening of our first kiss.

I'm finally in a long-term committed relationship, with a woman, her daughter, and our cats, and I've never felt more relaxed or more like I knew what I was doing. It's frightening to think that you could live an entire lifetime hiding something this important from yourself. It could hinge entirely on the chance that you'd meet the one person who could force it out of you and hand you the key to your happiness.

Geraldine's Story

She talked of her great desire for me, how it had taken her by surprise, how consuming it was. She was scaring the shit out of me.

Two years ago, at age forty, after a life of frequent, short-lived, and generally unsatisfactory liaisons with males, I resigned myself to celibacy. I relied for companionship on a few close female friends. I persuaded myself that what I'd lost in this lifestyle was compensated for by the lack of stress I felt.

Though my friends all griped constantly about their men, they bemoaned just as regularly my lack of "a man in my life." We even joked about their misery-loves-company attitudes.

Then things changed in a big way. One of the women I worked with, Olivia, a quiet widow I didn't know well, brought a friend to our company potluck. Her friend, a younger woman of about thirty, was introduced as Jamie. Throughout the dinner and afterwards, I noticed Jamie staring at me, though she didn't say a word to me the whole time. I had a hard time enjoying myself, knowing that any time I looked her way, she would catch my gaze and return it. A couple of times she smiled. It was unsettling. I wasn't sure why.

As the party broke up and I was scraping dishes, Jamie stayed behind while Olivia went to her car.

"Hi," Jamie said to me. "I'm Jamie Sutherland. Gerry, right?"

"Hi." I took her hand. "Yes, you're a friend of Olivia's."

She nodded. "You interest me, Gerry. Could we have lunch sometime?"

Shocked at her boldness, I stuttered.

"Thursday?" she suggested.

"Uh, okay," I said, not really sure why I agreed.

Our lunch lasted until 3 o' clock, at which time I called my boss and told him my car had broken down and I'd had to have it towed to a garage. Jamie and I talked for two more hours in my car outside her apartment building. On my way home, I was amazed to realize that I'd agreed to dinner on Saturday.

Saturday night we closed the place at one in the morning. I don't remember what we talked about for all those hours. I just remember being unable to escape this force. Jamie seemed to have some sort of power over me.

She started dropping by after work, sometimes with Chinese food or sandwiches. She soon made it clear that she was sexually attracted to me. I was alarmed. "I'm not a lesbian," I told her.

But I was under her spell. She talked of her great desire for me, how it had taken her by surprise, how consuming it was. She was scaring the shit out of me.

She began to touch me, holding my hand, kissing my cheek, pushing the hair from my face. A few days later she was kissing me on the mouth and fondling my breasts, and I liked it. I began to relax, to welcome this new kind of physical pleasure.

But it was moving very fast. I had known her less than a month when she persuaded me to go to bed. I still wasn't sure what was happening to me, wasn't sure I wanted it to happen. But the passionate hours we spent together were wonderful.

I asked her to spend the night, but she would always leave before morning, and I noticed that most weekends she wasn't free to be with me. She never invited me to her apartment either, which I found puzzling. When I questioned her about it, she said she didn't want Olivia to know she was sleeping with a woman. At the time, that made sense to me.

It makes even more sense now. She didn't want Olivia to know she was sleeping with "another" woman.

Meanwhile, I was overwhelmed by the passion and the power of this attraction. I wanted more. I asked Jamie to move in. She hedged. In light of the incredible sex, I was confused and hurt by her reluctance to make a commitment to me.

Then she dropped the bomb. She and Olivia had found a house to buy. They were moving in together. They'd apparently been planning this for some time. I was angry and unable to believe it. Jamie said that she couldn't give me up, that we could go on as before. She said that Olivia knew nothing about our affair.

I'm ashamed to say that we tried out this plan of deception for a few weeks, but I always felt that, except for sex, I didn't matter as much to Jamie as she did to me. In a final difficult act of self-respect, I told her it was over, this whirlwind of passion which had swept away my senses.

My humiliation over this betrayal, more blatant than any I'd experienced with a man, made me swear myself again to celibacy. I think I'd always known how to handle men, how to distance myself, emotionally. I had fallen into it completely with Jamie.

After a couple of years, my wounds have begun to heal. I've begun to recall with regret the missing passion in my life and have resolved to give loving a woman another chance. This time, when I find her, I expect to be a little less susceptible to awe, and a little more under control. Now I know myself better, and I know what it means to love a woman.

Doreen's Story

Over the next year she kept pushing me away, but when I would leave her alone for a while, she'd show up at my house and take me to bed.

When I was forty-five I was seduced by an office friend, Linda, who controls all of the people in her life through sex. But I didn't know that at the time. She seduced me slowly, over a period of time, by telling me she loved me, telling me how important I was to her, kissing me frequently, first just on the cheek, and then, as time went by, on the mouth too.

One night when I was consoling Linda over a problem, she kissed me very passionately and took me to bed and made love to me. She was my first woman, but I wasn't hers.

Over the next year she kept pushing me away, but when I would leave her alone for a while, she'd show up at my house and take me to bed. It was crazy. I finally broke loose, though, from Linda.

At that point, I didn't know what had attracted me most about our affair. Was it loving a woman or was it just this woman? I went looking for number two to find out. I fell in love again. After more than two years, we're still together, but her drinking and moodiness are destroying us.

I probably won't stay in this relationship. When it's over, I plan to stay alone for a while. I've been in love four times in my life, twice with men, but I won't be with someone who makes me unhappy, regardless of gender.

Blythe's Story

She seduced me, deliberately and methodically, over a period of five years.

I'm not sure if I'm a lesbian or not, and I'm not much concerned with labeling myself, but I freely admit never before having had such an intimate, sharing, and sexually satisfying relationship. I hope Wendy stays around and continues to love me, but if she doesn't, I'm grateful for her persistence and the time we've had together.

She seduced me, deliberately and methodically, over a period of five years. I resisted for several reasons—she was too young (twenty-five to my fifty-three), I didn't trust the permanence of her love, I feared society's disapproval, I didn't want to influence her in her search for her true sexual identity, I didn't think I could reconcile my personal morality with lesbianism.

We practically lived together after my husband died. Wendy cooked all my dinners and spent every evening with me. We took weekend trips together and even got groceries together. About the only thing we didn't do together was sleep. I became very dependent on her, and I never denied loving her, but I insisted that it was a maternal love, not a sexual one.

She pushed me for sex, threw tantrums, tried to sneak up on me when she thought I'd be too tired or too drunk to resist. When she massaged my shoulders, it was relaxing. When she kissed my neck, it was pleasant. I felt vague sexual stirrings, but suppressed them.

Wendy had never had a female lover. If there was a possibility that she could be a heterosexual, I didn't want to be responsible for sidetracking her. She pleaded with me, making melodramatic declarations of eternal love. She's too young, I kept telling myself. She's got a crush.

After five years of trying and making little progress, Wendy was frustrated (desperate, probably). She began searching for a lover. She met a forty-five year old woman who succumbed to her seduction with a mere whimper of a struggle. As their affair began, Wendy intensified her attempts to seduce me, as though she needed to confirm my resilience before giving up.

I don't know if it was her increased efforts, my own fear of losing her, or a recognition that she was going to be a lesbian with or without me, but one night I gave in, and found myself in the midst of a triangle. It took several months to sort this mess out, Wendy trying to be honorable all around. She gave up her new lover, eventually, and came to live with me.

When I hold her in the night, I feel very much at peace. My marriage was never this close nor this comfortable, though I think of it as a happy and healthy marriage. I loved my husband. Wendy and I have been together as lovers for four years. Her devotion has merely deepened, and I sometimes berate myself for having so little faith in her before. She's much mellower now, understandably.

I don't know if I could ever love another woman this way. Perhaps, if I'm lucky, I'll never have to consider that possibility.

Shelly's Story

I don't know how she managed it, but somewhere between my handing her a tissue to dry her eyes and our labia interleaving, she seduced me.

The way I feel about it now is that I'm glad it happened, grateful in fact. At the time, I felt taken advantage of, at least at first. I had no idea Karen was a lesbian. She was my son's pediatrician, a woman I respected and admired. I had always had this thing about successful, independent women, so I was sort of in awe of her. My son Derek loved her. I wouldn't say he would fake an illness to see her, but it made the symptoms much easier to bear.

By the time Derek was sixteen, Karen and I had known each other almost as long, on a professional basis. It was 1986 and I had filed for divorce. When I took Derek in for a baseball injury, I remember Karen looking at me oddly and asking me if I felt okay.

When she'd finished with Derek, she asked to speak to me privately in her office. She said that Derek seemed depressed and surly, that she'd never seen him like this. And I looked like shit. What's up, she asked. I told her about the divorce. Up to that moment, I'd been holding up remarkably well, I thought. I was making decisions and acting on them rationally and responsibly, but it was all taking its toll. So there was this sympathetic woman, listening. Nobody else had been listening. Or maybe I just hadn't been willing to talk. I dumped all over her. I cried. She comforted me.

The next day she called me and asked how I was. I was so touched by this attention. What I didn't know was that she had always been attracted to me, but that the barrier of our professional liaison had prevented her from acknowledging it. Something changed after that day in her office. Perhaps after years of neglect by my husband, I was pretty easily won over by a kind word. I was thrilled, actually, that someone would take time out of her busy, important day to think of my welfare. I'd always thought she was wonderful with Derek, but now I just thought she was wonderful.

One day she asked me to go to dinner with her, noting that we'd known each other for sixteen years and had never even shared a cup of coffee. I was flattered. That night I learned that she'd never been married, and we talked about my husband, about my failed marriage. She was incredibly easy to talk to. I had a wonderful time, and back home afterwards, I felt exhilarated. I worried, however, that I'd dominated the conversation with my boring domestic problems and that an educated, fascinating woman like Karen would find me far too dull to waste any more time on.

But she called again, and invited me to her condo for a Saturday night dinner. I wonder sometimes how I could have been so dense not to have seen the nature of her interest. I was probably just too wrapped up in myself. And I'd never known a lesbian. I'd never had a woman interested that way. It didn't occur to me to even think of it.

She prepared a lovely dinner and we drank wine. I was having a marvelous time. Karen talked about opera, one of her passions, and talked about it in a hilarious way. I knew nothing about opera, but it was really funny. Even though she loved it, she loved poking fun at it just as much.

I wasn't used to drinking, and three glasses of wine made me silly. We both giggled too much. After dinner, sitting in the living room, Karen took me in her arms and kissed me, kissed me ardently, like a man might. I was shocked. I pushed her away, my mind in turmoil.

She came after me, holding me down, pinning me beneath her on the sofa. I wasn't afraid of her, not like I would have been if she'd been a man. I mean, I wasn't afraid of physical violence. She kissed me again, more gently, on the corner of the mouth. I just lay there, stunned.

"Shelly," she said, "I'm crazy about you. The first time you walked into my office, I thought to myself, Oh, God, please let this woman be a lesbian. Well, your information sheet dashed that fantasy." She told me that the way I looked at her, the way I'd been responding these past few weeks, she was sure that I understood, that I too felt the attraction. I told her I didn't. I told her she was wrong. She let me loose.

Then I felt really guilty because she seemed so disappointed and apologetic. In an effort to cheer her up, I stayed and talked. This time we talked about her life, about her painful homosexual adolescence, her failed relationships, the long-term lover she had split with a year earlier.

I felt like I was way out of my depth trying to comfort Karen. I had no reference point for what she was talking about, but gradually I began to see the human aspect of it more than the sexual one, and I realized there wasn't much difference between her pain and my own.

I think I succumbed out of sympathy, then, to her caresses. I felt very close to her, and I still felt flattered by her interest, maybe even more so after learning that it was sexual. I don't know how she managed it, but somewhere between my handing her a tissue to dry her eyes and our labia interleaving, she seduced me.

Karen, I found out, was an incredibly demanding woman. She wanted me to belong to her. But she was a gentle, generous, and untiring lover. For several months I overlooked her jealousy and moodiness to enjoy the pleasures of her bed.

She certainly helped me overcome my doubts about the divorce. When I kissed Karen, I couldn't even question that decision. My marriage had been like a mausoleum. When I made love with Karen, my body screamed with life.

I didn't want to give her up, but we really weren't suited to one another, temperamentally. When at last I convinced myself, through involvement in my local lesbian community, that there were other women in the world who might be able to love me, I broke off my affair with Derek's lovely pediatrician.

I haven't been interested in men since. I've had two other affairs with women, and am searching for Ms. Right. Karen and I see each other from time to time. I have to admit that the spark is still there. Three times since our breakup, we've ended up in bed with each other. But she now has a live-in lover, so we control ourselves. I really hope that this one works out for her, and I know she'll feel the same for me when the time comes.

2

Gradual Awakening

It's easy to say now I was always a lesbian, but it wasn't something I wanted to know.

It was as though I'd seen myself clearly for the first time in almost fifty years of living.

I wasn't able to face my sexual identity until I'd peeled back years and layers of conditioning and started becoming who I really am.

I now realize that I've had lots of crushes, and many women who would have been lovers had I known it was possible.

*   *   *

This is by far the best populated category. I've included both women who were relieved with their awakening and those who were appalled or frightened by it.

For these women, a series of images and suggestions occurred over many years. Their desire for women was awakened through observation, by movies, books, observing lesbian couples, or being exposed to lesbians, and thereby recognizing something about themselves.

They often describe clues that they didn't recognize at the time, but now see as evidence that their coming out had occurred over many years. Most of them believe that lesbianism was lurking in them all along, waiting for the time to be right. They describe their earlier sexuality as a false mask hiding the "truth" from others and themselves.

If lesbianism can be thought of as a truth for these women, it's easy to see why, once known, it can no longer be denied, though some of these women deserve a commendation for their attempts. Though often resisted, truth has a tendency to win out in the end.

Women who were actively seduced by lesbians are not included here, but knowing or becoming friends with lesbians, as in the other chapters, was often a factor in prompting their awakening.

Toni's Story

Somewhere deep inside me, I knew the truth. But I would have denied it to God.

Every time we pulled up stakes following my husband's latest career move, I had to tear myself apart from a dear female friend. This time it had been Joanie, perhaps the dearest of them all. Saying goodbye to her had been heartbreaking.

I took a job as a secretary in our new home in California. I usually worked, but because of all the moving, I'd never had a career and never got paid much. I resolved not to get close to anyone this time. I didn't want the pain of a separation. If you stay in a place long enough, natural human bonds begin to form, whether you plan them or not. By the end of a year, I was making friends at work. But I carefully avoided extending those relationships outside of work.

Despite my intended precautions, I began to get very close to the budget analyst, Debbie. She was an interesting woman, thirty-four, highly intelligent, with numerous talents and a sarcastic sense of humor. By the time I started telling Debbie my most private thoughts, it began to look like my family was settling into a permanent home.

Debbie was very private, listening empathetically to whatever I had to say, but volunteering little about herself. She could speak on any subject, and we had some vehement religious, social, and political discussions.

Over many months we became closer and closer, and I began to suspect that Debbie was a lesbian. She spoke of a former female friend named Emily with a strange sort of longing. And once, after a visit to see Emily, she appeared emotionally devastated. She was reluctant to discuss it, but the clues were piling up. In discussions about homosexuality, during which I voiced my disapproval, Debbie was uncharacteristically noncommittal.

Debbie had no history of men, either, and never spoke of them as something to be desired. By the time I started figuring this out, our friendship was far too involved to be ended. Besides, I didn't want to end it, even if she was a lesbian. Perhaps, I thought, this is an opportunity to learn something, and with the growing interest in the general population, I was beginning to realize that I probably deserved the uncomfortable label of bigot." I think I thought Debbie could redeem me, teach me tolerance, in my heart, not just outwardly. I liked her. She was perfectly normal. If this was a bonafide lesbian, I thought, I knew I could work through my homophobia.

The next time the subject of Debbie's mysterious friend came up, I asked the question that plunged us over the edge. "Were the two of you lovers?"

By now there wasn't a chance that either of us could lie to the other. She told me the story of her affair and breakup. For the next several weeks, the subject of Debbie's sexuality wasn't far from our discussions. A whole new part of her life had been opened up, and I realized how constricted she'd been with me before. I had been thinking of us as extremely close friends, but her heart had been almost entirely unknown to me. We became closer.

I started calling Debbie at the end of every workday, regardless of how much we'd seen of each other, to wish her a pleasant evening. When Friday came, I felt desperate, knowing we wouldn't see one another until Monday. If anything more important than a hang nail happened in my life, I called her to tell her.

We began parting with hugs. I was utterly oblivious to my growing dependence. This was just another of those intense friendships, I told myself. It had happened before. It was normal . . . for me. Maybe I shouldn't let it be so important, but what was the harm? Somehow I knew there was harm, though. Some days I found myself trying to resist the desire to call her.

While all of this was going on with me, it was exactly the same for her. We were falling in love. Debbie knew it. I didn't. I was going around patting myself on the back for being such good friends with a lesbian, saying things like, "The reason I don't feel threatened by you is that I'm so secure in my own sexual identity." Today I can laugh at that.

Debbie and I started seeing each other away from work, going to lunch, going shopping. She took up coaching my son in tennis. I didn't tell my husband or my son that my new best friend was a lesbian. I suppose I occasionally expressed the fear that Debbie might become sexually attracted to me, so she continued to assure me that that wasn't going to happen. Everything was cool, she said. Good, I said. Meanwhile she was fantasizing like hell about me.

I learned through knowing Debbie that she wasn't the only lesbian I knew. My doctor was a lesbian. The woman who did my hair was a lesbian. Debbie was teaching me how to tell, and she had made me hypersensitive to the entire subject. I argued for homosexual rights in my Bible study class, which put me at odds with several members. When someone at work made an insensitive joke about gays, I told him I didn't think it was funny. I was proud of my new tolerance.

Somewhere deep inside me, I knew the truth. But I would have denied it to God. This went on for two years. Sometimes Debbie teased me, like the time we went shopping, and on the way home from the mall, she said, "Why don't you turn off here and we can go out in the country and make out." We both laughed.

It was getting harder and harder for Debbie, though. Finally she gave in. One Saturday over a table at one of our favorite restaurants, she took hold of my hand and looked at me with a deep gaze.

"I'm in love with you, Toni," she said. "I know you know that on some level, and I know you feel the same way. I'm bringing this out in the open because I can't go on like this, denying my desire for you."

I pulled my hand away, shocked. I suppose I literally ran away. Debbie tried to talk to me over the next couple of weeks, bullying me about hiding my head in the sand and lying to myself.

I told her she was wrong, very wrong. I told her I could never love her or any other woman that way, and I was adamant. I told her that our friendship was over, unless . . . . (Of course I couldn't let her go. I was in love with her. Not knowing it didn't make much difference, did it?) I told her our friendship was over unless she never mentioned love again and didn't act on her feelings.

"Do you understand?" I asked her.

"Oh, yes," she said, "I understand perfectly."

Much better than I did, obviously.

Our friendship continued, but I put an end to the hugs, though they had never been sexual. When Debbie started distancing herself from me, an understandable attempt at self-preservation, I began to panic. I invited her to a play because I knew she liked theater. At first she said no, but then she said yes.

The play was mediocre, or maybe I just couldn't concentrate on it. Debbie sat beside me in the dark, our arms occasionally brushing together. I was so conscious of her physical presence that I felt I'd been through an emotionally draining experience by the time I drove her home.

I stopped the car outside her apartment house.

"Toni," she said, "shut off the engine a moment. I have something to say to you."

Uh, oh, I thought. In the still dark night, we sat facing each other.

"I know I promised not to mention . . . love, but I'm not going to be able to keep this up. It's too difficult. I need to move on, break away from these emotions. We aren't going to be able to be friends, just friends."

She told me she loved me and was sorry that I couldn't reciprocate. She told me she understood the fear. Then she leaned towards me and kissed me on the mouth, softly, lingering for a moment.

"Goodbye," she whispered.

As my lips felt the memory of hers, she left the car and in a flash was up the concrete stairway and into her apartment. A light appeared in the window. Tears ran down my cheeks. What would I do without Debbie, I thought, desperate. I sat there in my car, bewildered.

And, then, feeling stupid for not having said anything, I left the car parked at the curb and ran upstairs. I knocked on her door. When she opened it, I invited myself in. Debbie had already changed her clothes. She wore a long nightshirt which reached nearly to her knees. Her feet were bare.

"We have to talk," I said melodramatically.

"There's nothing to talk about," she said.

"I think there is. I don't want to stop being friends. I need you."

"You don't understand, Toni. I sat next to you this evening without for a moment being able to forget you were there, wanting desperately to hold your hand. I have to keep telling myself no. It's painful. Why should I subject myself to that?"

"I wouldn't have minded if you held my hand," I said, near tears.

She shook her head. "It goes further, of course. Look, here we are alone in my apartment. I'm resisting right now, resisting holding you, kissing you. If I see you, I want you."

As she said those words, a warm ray of lust moved through my chest, down through my stomach. I stood there dumbly, staring at her. The frown on her face gradually disappeared as we stood there, just stood there saying nothing. I could hear a voice inside me, saying, "Hold me, kiss me. I want you too."

As if Debbie could hear that silent voice, eventually she moved towards me, then put her arms around me quite slowly. I felt my body tremble as she touched her lips to mine. Her kisses were tender and thorough, causing surges of desire to course through me. She pressed herself against me. I could feel her loose breasts against mine, the soft roundness of them most alluring.

I couldn't believe what I was feeling. I kissed her hungrily, with a need I'd never known before, holding her tighter and tighter. Eventually she took me to her bed, and we made love all night, spurred on by an incredibly unrelenting passion.

After that night, I became obsessed with Debbie. I couldn't sleep. I couldn't eat. All I wanted was to be in her arms. There was never enough time, so few opportunities to be together. My need for Debbie overwhelmed everything else. I told my husband about her, and then I spent the next several months moving back and forth between them.

I went to a psychologist to get an objective voice to tell me I wasn't a lesbian and shouldn't let this obsession ruin my marriage and my life. I wanted to be told to give her up. Every time I gave her up, we spent hours on the phone explaining to each other what was wrong about our relationship and going over the details of our times together with a comic nostalgia.

By this time, there wasn't much worth saving in my marriage. I filed for divorce in May of 1991, and my husband moved out. Debbie moved in. She's still here. I'm so grateful to her for her patience and wisdom and maturity. She still knows me better than I do, and when required, she'll point me in the right direction.

Debbie says that I've always been a lesbian, and I suppose she's right. Realizing it was a painful process. But I'm so happy now that it was certainly worth it.

Roberta's Story

I'd been unclear and searching for a long time. Why couldn't someone help me out if they had known or suspected?

February 12, 1977 was so remarkable for me that I noted it in my journal as a day of reckoning. A PBS movie entitled "War Widow" aired that day. The protagonist of the movie, a recently widowed young mother, met a young female artist, with whom she fell in love.

The impact on me was immediate and revelatory. I realized that never before in my forty-three years had I felt a love story. I felt every look, every unsaid word and emotion of that movie, and when it had finished I said to myself in essence, "That's it. That's who I am. Tomorrow I begin from zero."

The following day I began writing to all the people whose friendships I treasured. I told them I realized at last who I was and that I was giving them the opportunity to continue being my friends or to choose not to. I was prepared for the worst and was pleasantly surprised that I'd lose very few friends.

The most discouraging thing was that several said, "I thought so," or, "I've known it for a long time." I'd been unclear and searching for a long time. Why couldn't someone help me out if they had known or suspected? I feel as if some of the best times of my life have gone down the proverbial drain and that I could have become so much more had the energy I'd wasted in wondering and perhaps denying been used for more productive things.

Once I accepted my orientation I felt that a load had been lifted off my shoulders. I also felt my energy becoming centered in myself, in my body, instead of being dispersed and fragmented.

Soon after, I searched out the Gay Community Center and someone introduced me to a few bars. I also discovered a lesbian group at NOW, and that's where I met my first lover.

Since then I've had two serious relationships. One of them was just a summer fling, but full and meaningful to me. The other lasted four years and the breakup was as painful as they get. As a result, I haven't until recently even considered looking for another meaningful relationship. But living the life I was meant for, although hard at times, has been worth it in the long run.

Diane's Story

For a long time, I now realized, I had put more worth on my relationships with women. I didn't associate this with lesbianism until I observed the intimate moments between Margie and Stacy.

Margie was dying. Her breast cancer had metastasized to the bone. She was in agony and we were administering powerful narcotics to help her endure. As the night nurse, I'd gotten to know her pretty well, first as a breast cancer patient, and now as a bone cancer patient. I liked Margie, and I liked her friend Stacy as well. Stacy came every day and spent hours by Margie's side, holding her hand, talking quietly with her. You could tell they were close. You could tell Stacy cared a great deal for her friend. I was grateful that Margie had someone like this, since she was unmarried and apparently had no family. She had a few others visitors, but it was Stacy who kept a loyal vigil.

I remember once envying the intimacy of these two and feeling ashamed over that, since one of them was dying and one of them was grief-stricken. But it was so touching and so sincere, and I couldn't relate it to anything in my own life. Even my ex-husband and I had never been that close, not even in the beginning when we were in love.

One evening I came upon Stacy in the hallway, a few doors down from Margie's room. She was sitting on a bench, sobbing into a Kleenex. I sat beside her and put a hand on her arm. She looked at me, tears streaking down her cheeks.

"I feel so fucking useless," she said.

I felt myself getting emotional then, and in a few moments we were crying all over each other.

If she felt useless, how did she think I felt? I was supposed to be able to do something. All I could do was relieve the pain so Margie could die with a minimum of agony.

The following night I attended Margie, who was only partly conscious and very near the end. She gripped my arm and said, "Stacy?"

"No," I said, "It's Diane. Stacy will probably be here in about fifteen minutes."

"Oh," she said, calm, but disappointed. Was she timing her death, I wondered. People did that. They waited until it was time. Somehow they could do that, as incredible as it seems, but I've seen daughters begging their mothers to wait just one more hour until their son arrives, and as soon as the son is there, affirming his presence, she dies. It can't always be coincidence.

"Don't give me any more of that stuff," Margie said, looking me in the eye. "I want to be awake when she comes."

Margie was only thirty-eight.

"Are you sure?" I asked, aware that the only job I had was relieving the pain.

"I'm sure. I want to feel it."

I bit my lip and withdrew the hypo I'd prepared to inject her with.

"Thank you, Diane," she said. "Thank you for being so helpful. I know this must be painful for you, too. Some people think that you get immune to suffering and death, but I can't believe that."

"No," I said, "I haven't, anyway. Maybe some do."

She patted my hand, as if I were the one needing comfort. Well, maybe I was. Her face was sallow and gray, her body almost lifeless, limp and weak, her muscles shrunken. But in the light of her eyes was the spirit of a woman with courage and intensity, a woman who shouldn't be dying.

I saw her staring into my eyes, transfixed almost, or trying to hypnotize me, maybe, but she stared and said nothing, and for a moment I thought she was dead, her fingers gripping my wrist. But then she blinked her eyes.

"Diane," she said weakly, "I want to tell you something important. Stacy and I are lovers. We've been together fifteen years. I want someone to understand what this means to her, losing me. She's going to be devastated. I feel so guilty for doing this to her."

Margie's tears cut through my own bias against what she was telling me, against homosexuality. At that moment, it almost didn't matter. I held her hand and reassured her that I understood.

But did I? I'd known some lesbians, from a distance. You can't be a nurse and not know some. But I'd never known them well. Now I understood Stacy's devotion, and I understood Margie's confession. She wanted someone to take responsibility for Stacy, to make sure she could cope.

Why me? I thought. People expect miracles while they're alive, but do they need to ask for miracles after they're dead? What could I do?

"I know you'll care," Margie said.

The trust she put in me was entirely a matter of faith. I didn't think I was worthy and didn't welcome the burden. Margie was merely desperate. There wasn't anyone else.

By now Margie was wracked with pain and enduring stoically. Stacy was overdue, so I sat beside the bed, holding Margie's hand, wanting to inject her with a medication that would practically knock her unconscious, but she wouldn't hear of it.

When Stacy arrived, I relinquished my position. Normally, we wouldn't allow visitors after eight o' clock, especially non-family visitors, but at midnight, Stacy was still there and I wasn't about to send her away.

Earlier in the evening I witnessed a tender kiss between them. Margie had told Stacy that I knew, so now they made no effort to hide their love for one another in my presence.

My shift ended at midnight, but I found myself lingering. I didn't want to leave when Margie's life was so precariously in the lurch. I told my relief nurse that I'd stay. If nothing else, this would relieve Stacy of the need to be cautious. Earlier, I'd seen her pull away from Margie when the doctor came in.

The bond between these two women was so intense and so absolute. Now that I knew its nature, I could appreciate the depth of feeling between them. Margie died at one-thirty in the morning. It was left to me to pull their hands apart.

I can't explain how touched I was by the tenderness of this love. As soon as Stacy's hand no longer held her lover's, she began to sob. I never responded before like I did that night to someone's anguish. I took her in my arms and held her, like a child, letting her cry into my shoulder. Stacy's sobs were wracking, gasping cries of loss.

Eventually I drove her home, and on the way she said more than once that she had nothing left to live for. I was afraid she would kill herself. Sometimes a few hours can mean the difference between suicide and stability, so I invited myself into their home and made Stacy take a couple of sleeping pills. I sat by her bed until she fell asleep.

Over the following days, Stacy and I got to know each other better, and I began to realize, through our many conversations about Margie, that my previous relationships with men seemed shallow in comparison. I know that all lesbian relationships are not ideal, but this one seemed to have been.

For a long time, I now realized, I had put more worth on my relationships with women. I didn't associate this with lesbianism until I observed the intimate moments between Margie and Stacy.

Stacy and I became good friends, and it was through her that I gradually came to realize my own attraction to women. She introduced me to other lesbians and lesbian organizations, and I'm now in a relationship with a woman, the most satisfying relationship of my life.

I'm grateful to Margie, a courageous woman who was tuned in enough to sense in me the potential for understanding that I was unaware of myself. God protect you, Margie. I'll always be inspired by your courage.

Peggy's Story

I spent many years trying to conform in other ways, so I'm sure that I could have fended off any lesbian feelings I might have had.

I recently had another talk (argument) with my oldest son. He supports my decision to be a lesbian for the most part, but he still believes I'm just "going through a phase." It's difficult for him to understand how I just CHANGED in my forties. I'm now fifty-one. At forty-seven, I finally knew I was a lesbian. At forty-nine, I had my first sexual encounter with a woman.

I told my son that it's possible that I was heterosexual for so many years because I was trying to do the right thing. I spent many years trying to conform in other ways, so I'm sure that I could have fended off any lesbian feelings I might have had.

I know I never fit in, that I never really enjoyed sex with men. The ones who did satisfy me, satisfied me only in a physical way. I can't remember feeling any intimacy, which I have now experienced with women.

I also discovered that I'm a very sexual person now that I'm loving women. I enjoyed sex with men to some degree, but after a while, the other stuff you had to go through wasn't worth the sex. I mean the fact that you almost always got treated like a second-class citizen. And most men are not generous lovers. I was celibate for ten years, and the three or four years prior to that, I slept with one man for physical release only.

Coming out so late has its special angles, especially since I'm divorced and have three children. People assume that I'm not only heterosexual but, because of my age and weight, asexual. People I work with assume I'm married or, if they know I'm not, seem to feel sorry for me because they assume I have no social life and certainly no sex life.

I remember last year when I was meeting someone right after work, so I had on makeup and was dressed a little fancier than usual. A male coworker passed me in the hall and said, slyly, "I'll bet it's a man." I smiled and said, "I'll bet you're wrong."

That gave me a bit of satisfaction because he was so smug about it. However, I was also angry, at both of us, him for his assumption, and me for not having the courage to tell him the truth. The important people in my life, though, my family and close friends, know.

Another thing that feels strange is to be older and wiser about everything but lesbian life. I feel too mature for most of the women I've dated, yet I feel like a greenhorn in terms of relationships and sex with women.

In addition to coming to it late, I'm also faced with the added difficulty of being African American, which makes my personal lesbian community harder to find, even in a metropolitan area.

I fantasize, from time to time, about having sex with lots of women, sequentially, not all at once, because I enjoy sex with women so much.

The best thing about what's happened to me is that I often find myself bursting with happiness and being as giddy as a schoolgirl. Perhaps it's just as well that I came to this life when I was old enough and mature enough (almost) to handle it.

Lisa's Story

I now realize that I was never attracted to boys or men, and I've had lots of crushes on women that I thought were cases of hero worship.

Ever since I was a small child, I have been aware that I think and feel differently from the accepted norm. Growing up in a ranch family with three older brothers who ceaselessly told me that girls "can't do that" made me determined to do what I wanted to prove to myself that I'm as good as a male.

I hated feminine clothes, and to this day I feel uncomfortable wearing them. As for penis envy, the only time I have it is when I can't pee out in the country as males do.

Since I always felt I could never (didn't want to) be a "normal" woman, I planned to be a biologist and not ever a wife.

However, as a freshman in college, I fell in love with the cowboy who was pursuing me relentlessly and dropped out to become a ranch wife. I tried to do what was expected, but I also worked on the ranch, probably harder than my husband. We had two sons, and I taught them how to ride and all the ranch stuff, as well as supervised their school work and activities. Still, all the while I felt that I wasn't a good wife and mother.

When my husband became an alcoholic, I finally figured out that I didn't want to go down the tubes with him. I returned to college and got my B.S. in agriculture. I was something of a pioneer (for women) in this field and was highly successful. Ten years later I got my Master's.

I now realize that I was never attracted to boys or men, and I've had lots of crushes on women that I thought were cases of hero worship. It never occurred to me that I might be a lesbian. When my lover came into my life eight years ago, she had to show me. In looking back, I can see that there were many women who were interested in a love relationship with me. I didn't notice because I had resigned myself to being asexual. It hadn't occurred to me that a lesbian relationship was an option.

By the time my lover came along, I was ready for her, having opened up to the possibility through friendships with lesbians, particularly lesbian couples, and through a greater appreciation of myself.

Vickie's Story

What was most stunning was the incredible power of the sexual energy which flowed between us. I remember trying to suppress it, deny it, explain it away. After all, I was a "happily" married woman.

My journey of discovering my lesbianism was a coming together of many forces and processes, a function of circumstances and, I believe, my inner preparedness. During my twenty-year marriage, I progressively found myself wanting more out of the relationship and in my life as a whole. My dissatisfaction began a few years after I married, but the relationship continued with a veneer of being traditional and happy. I coped with my anxieties by overworking; my husband did the same. Meanwhile we raised two beautiful boys.

I read self-help books and talked to my mother about my troubles. I thought I had "the problem," whatever "the problem" was.

My husband and I were an agreeable couple who had no life crises to manage. You could say we were "lucky." As the years went by, I worked, raised the kids, got a masters degree, and when the boys were old enough, went to work full time.

As my confidence grew, my earnings also increased, and I became more satisfied with my career. I ultimately took a directorship of a school of nursing. I earned almost as much as my husband and was very successful. It now seemed that I had control of my professional life.

During this time I began feeling attractions to women at work. I didn't know if it was their intellect, articulateness, sensitivity, playfulness, or my own openness to experiencing women on a new level, but the feelings were definitely sexual.

During all my married years, the only reading material that gave me inspiration, hope, comfort, and insight was *Ms. Magazine.* It talked about lesbians—I was curious. It talked about strong women—I was curious.

This was when I met Marty, my first (and still only) female lover. It was the first time for her, too. She was a thirty-three year old student in my nursing program. During her stay at the college, we became close, as teacher and student, advisor and advisee, and eventually as friends. After nine or ten months I knew there as an attraction between us, but I kept it to myself.

What was most stunning was the incredible power of the sexual energy which flowed between us. I remember trying to suppress it, deny it, explain it away. After all, I was a "happily" married woman.

I initiated the physical relationship. When we started to make love it was like what romance novels describe, but better. Beyond words, I experienced rapture.

I'd loved before, but now I was a captive of the love, sex, and passion. I was overwhelmed by the sex—satisfying, passionate, spiritual, sizzling, tender, and the adjectives go on.

I hadn't before known multiple orgasm. It would go on for hours, days, on and on. I was addicted. But I was also guilt-ridden. I kept Marty secret for several months, and then I told my husband. Neither of us coped well.

The messy phase of my life began, continuing for years. I went to counseling, tried to give Marty up, then tried to see her platonically. That was like being thirsty all the time. For a long while, we had an on again, off again relationship. My counselor characterized it as an addiction.

Since Marty, I haven't been attracted to a man. I'm now divorced. My boys are okay with Marty, but we don't talk about the relationship as a lesbian one. Marty and I are exploring the possibility of living together. I am the cautious one.

Experiencing a lesbian relationship was and is a meaningful learning experience. It came as part of my mid-life crisis and continues to push me into a self-examination direction. Expanding my sexual horizons is part of it. I will continue to seek out the growth possibilities in my relationship with Marty.

Sandy's Story

I started retracing the events of my life. I was startled to realize that I had always loved women, that in fact I'd been in love with several women throughout my life.

It took an awfully long time. I'm forty-seven now, and only within the past year have I established a sexual relationship with a woman. It is totally wonderful and I wish I hadn't wasted so much of my life with men, trying to please them and be with them.

I got married when I was twenty-six, after six years of being sexually active with men. My marriage lasted seventeen years. He was handsome, intelligent, we had a lot in common, and I enjoyed sex with him. I wasn't in love, but I liked him a lot. I never felt a real communion with him. There always seemed to be something preventing a real relationship. Eventually, my marriage seemed kind of dead.

When I was thirty-eight, I met a woman at work. I fell madly and passionately in love with Julia almost immediately. We became friends. I couldn't understand what was happening to me.

I thought about her constantly. I dreamed about her. Every time the phone rang I hoped it was her, and when it was, it was like I just melted, every time. I never got tired of her or bored or annoyed. I would get so excited and nervous whenever I'd get to see her that I would breathe erratically and perspire. It was crazy, especially for me, ordinarily a stable, non-neurotic, calm person. I tried to regain control of myself. No use.

Then I started having intensely erotic dreams about Julia. They were beautiful and wonderful, so much more meaningful than anything I'd ever experienced with men. This really scared me, and I determined to drop the relationship. I didn't talk to Julia or see her for two years.

During this time my marriage fell apart and I got divorced. All along I couldn't stop thinking and dreaming about Julia. Finally, we reconciled, as friends. Ultimately, she moved out of state. I was both sad and relieved, as it was extremely frustrating to be "just friends." But I really loved her and missed her terribly.

I tried dating men for a while, but it was the same old unsatisfying thing. I decided that maybe it was time to consider the possibility that I was a lesbian. It was hard for me to accept this, but I felt that I just didn't fit into the mainstream, and I was very lonely.

I started retracing the events of my life. I was startled to realize that I had always loved women, that in fact I'd been in love with several women throughout my life. I had just thought of them as "deep relationships" and had never before thought of the sexual possibilities with women.

Still not sure of who I was, I joined a correspondence club for lesbians. Several women wrote to me, giving me support and encouragement. I found out that I'm far from the only one who has lived this particular drama. I couldn't believe the love and encouragement I received. It literally changed my perception of the world. I met Laurie about a year ago through this organization. We're lovers now, and it's so wonderful that it's beyond verbal description. The transition between being sexual with men and being with a woman was so easy that I wondered why I had ever worried about it. It just seemed so natural. I've never felt so happy, so at home, so at peace with myself.

It's so wonderful to be truly intimate with someone, and to be free to express that love. I will never go back to men. I don't hate men, but they're like aliens to me.

I feel sorry for my heterosexual girlfriends who are eternally seeking and never finding in a man what I've found in a woman. I feel very fortunate that life has given me this wonderful gift. Thanks to all the women out there who have had the courage to follow your hearts. You have trailblazed for me, and led me to the heart center. I'm very grateful.

3

Lucy and Ethel

We'd probably loved each other for years, but it took a pitcher of margaritas and a Monty Python television marathon to push us over that last hurdle.

Naomi was the best friend I'd ever had. I was terrified that these sexual feelings would destroy our friendship.

In the morning we both started screaming rape and accusing each other, but after breakfast, we decided to take a bubble bath together.

*   *   *

Into this section fall the women who had no prior attraction to women, who seemed the typical wives and mothers, or in some cases, single career women. Their first lesbian experience came with another heterosexual woman, a friend who may also have been taken off guard by the physical attraction.

Usually, the realization of sexual desire came gradually. Often it was triggered by an outside stimulus, and was frequently accompanied by alcohol or an erotic environment.

Usually, these women didn't identify themselves as lesbians after their first sexual encounter. They felt instead that they had succumbed to circumstances, and the experience could be dismissed as unimportant, a temporary weakness.

This type of lesbian experience happens to many heterosexual women, often with no lasting propensity towards lesbianism. With these women, however, things were different. The lesbian experience touched some hidden chord in them and released a suppressed desire. It was the first step towards a future lesbian life.

Carol's Story

We lapsed into silence then, finishing the beers, me, probably both of us, thinking about what it'd be like to make it with a woman.

It all started with the movie *The Color Purple*, which Lois and I rented on a Saturday night because her husband was out of town for the weekend. Mine was living in a tiny apartment downtown, having moved out two months earlier. Lois and I had been friends for years, had helped each other through crisis after crisis, had talked over cups of coffee about faked orgasms, sagging breasts, Tom Selleck, and all of the issues of our lives.

My son had even dated Lois's oldest daughter briefly, a trying experience for our friendship. In our forties, we talked each other through more serious problems with our marriages. Mine had come apart. Lois and her husband Sam were trying to patch things up after his latest affair.

With her youngest child now in college, Lois was alone in the house that weekend. She invited me over to watch a movie. She made popcorn and we drank beer, sitting on the floor of their family room amid a nest of pillows.

It was a good movie, powerful and moving. Lois always cried at movies, and this was no exception. The box of Kleenex was strategically placed behind us.

When Celie and Shug kissed, I felt it deep in my abdomen. I turned to Lois who stared glassy-eyed at me. How many beers has she had, I asked myself.

When the movie was over, Lois rewound the tape and stumbled into the kitchen to get us each another beer. We settled into the pillows.

"What'd you think?" Lois asked.

"I thought it was good."

"What'd you think of the two women getting together like that?"

"The men weren't worth much, so it made sense, I guess."

"Most men aren't worth much," Lois said, echoing an ongoing sentiment we expressed freely with one another, typical of straight women with men.

"No," I agreed.

"She didn't know what an orgasm was. Fucked hundreds of times and didn't know what an orgasm was. Can you believe it?"

"Sure."

Lois's speech was slurred. She was obviously drunk. "What do you think it's like?"

"What?"

"Sex with a woman?"

I shrugged. "I guess at least you'd have an orgasm. I guess."

"Yeah, probably. Nothing to go limp on you."

We lapsed into silence then, finishing the beers, me, probably both of us, thinking about what it'd be like to make it with a woman. When I looked again at Lois, she lay on her side, hand propping up her head, staring at me. She just stared, an odd expression on her face. After a moment, she said, "Kiss me."

"What?" I asked, puzzled.

"Kiss me."

Boy, is she drunk, I thought. Then I leaned down and kissed her, a light touch of my lips to hers. Her arms went around my neck and she dragged me down to her.

We made love there on the floor, on the pillows. We finger-fucked each other, then fell asleep. When I woke, Lois was in the kitchen brewing coffee. Slowly I remembered what had happened. I was feeling ill, and sleeping on the floor had left me with an aching back.

"Morning," Lois said, smiling.

After an Alka Seltzer and one cup of coffee, I said, "Do you remember last night?"

She nodded obliquely.

"Well?" I asked.

"We were drunk. It was just one of those things. It doesn't mean anything. Forget about it."

I nodded, unsure. "Okay. It never happened."

But I had a hard time forgetting about it. I kept remembering the feel of her warm pussy sliding over my fingers.

For the next few months, our friendship followed its usual course. The incident wasn't mentioned. I began dating a man from work, Robert, and soon he was sleeping over.

In October, we prepared for an annual tradition, a costume ball at the police station where Sam worked. This year Robert would be my date, and we decided on a Robin Hood theme. I was Robin Hood, Lois was Maid Marian, Sam would be the Sheriff of Nottingham, and Robert would go as Friar Tuck. Unfortunately, Robert required almost no adornment to fit his part of the bald, portly churchman.

A week before the event, I asked Lois to stop by my house to try on her gown. I was the seamstress of the group, so it was my job to make the costumes.

She twirled around in the shimmering sea green, medieval dress, her bosom protruding at the top.

"You need more of this," I said, pushing her breasts up and together. "You need a more bosomy look. I'll pad the bodice a bit."

Looking at her breasts reminded me of our drunken cavorting. I wasn't drunk now, but I felt drawn to her, aroused by her closeness.

I moved away. "So what do you think?"

"It's lovely. Is Sam's done?"

"Yes. Take it with you and have him try it."

I unzipped the gown and slipped it down over her body, leaving her in her slip. I carefully laid the dress on the end of the bed, then turned to see Lois standing there watching me. The look on her face wasn't unlike the look she'd given me that night when she asked me to kiss her. Almost against my will, I stepped towards her. I felt flushed and confused. I slipped the strap off her shoulder, then kissed it at the spot right inside the muscle. Her skin was soft. I pressed my cheek to her neck. I felt her hand on the back of my head.

When I tried to kiss her mouth, she turned away. "No," she said. "No, no, please."

She practically ran away, then, dressing in haste and bolting. I was thoroughly confused. Why was she trying to seduce me . . . and why was I responding?

This incident pretty much ended our friendship. There were overtures and pretenses and lots of excuses. After a while, we didn't see each other anymore. We exchange Christmas cards, that's about it. Now, since I've become a lesbian, Lois blames the whole thing on me, but she forgives me, she says.

I broke up with Robert after the Halloween party. I had never really liked him anyway. Looking back, I think he was just an excuse, a reaction to my desire for Lois.

Becoming a lesbian wasn't easy for me. It took several years and professional counseling. I hid from my attraction to women, and I denied it.

It's been three years since Lois and I watched *The Color Purple*. I've begun a relationship with a young woman who's incredibly patient and kind. I believe I'm falling in love. It feels very natural. Scary, too, but worth the risk. I adore making love with her. I adore everything about her. I've never felt more comfortable with another person. I'm envisioning old age with her. Even if it doesn't come to that, I'm hooked. I'm a lover of women.

Lana's Story

One time, after we came back to her apartment after a night out, we sat up talking about that pussy-eating woman.

Penny and I used to hang out together on Friday and Saturday nights. We'd become buddies in college, she a girl in her twenties, me a divorcee of forty-two. For some reason, we got along great. Sometimes we went to bars and flirted with guys. We protected each other when the guys got belligerent. I don't think either of us ever really wanted to pick a guy up. We just enjoyed the game.

We went to see the Chippendales a couple of times too. We talked about sex a lot. We compared our experiences. Penny had more, even though she was so much younger than me.

One night I asked her if she'd ever done it with a woman. She said she'd had her pussy eaten by a woman once. She said it had been a blast. Sometimes, when I was horny, I asked her to tell me about it, about how it felt and all.

One time, after we came back to her apartment after a night out, we sat up talking about that pussy-eating woman. I asked Penny if she had really liked it. She said yes. She said no man had ever licked her pussy like that. I was feeling awfully generous towards Penny those days. I asked her if she wanted me to do it to her. So we ended up eating each other. I liked it both ways, giving and getting.

Penny and I started staying in on Friday and Saturday nights. Now we stay in most nights. She's moved in with me and we're devoted to one another. All that flirting and guy watching was probably overcompensation, just an excuse to get horny together, probably.

Carmen's Story

I begged Pat to continue our affair, but she said her marriage was more important. It was just sex, after all, she said.

It's been a year now since I had my first sexual experience with a woman. I still feel pretty much devastated by it and am not really looking for someone new. I have a feeling, though, that if I ever fall for another woman, she'll be a lumberjack (or is it lumberjill?).

My best friend Pat and I decided to make some extra money by selling firewood last fall, only one of our many business ventures. We could afford to fail, both being married to successful professional men. But we expected to succeed, every time.

We'd tried a deli, a diet center, a second-hand clothing store, and hadn't lost too much money, ultimately. In the process, we'd learned a lot and had a lot of fun. Pat and I were clearly in it for the fun, though we told our husbands it was serious business.

Neither of them thought the firewood idea would work, ascribing such a business to the domain of men. But all you really needed to know how to do was wield a chain saw and drive a truck. My uncle had forty acres of wild oaks and apple orchard in the foothills of California, just an hour's drive from our urban sprawl.

We started in August, in the blistering heat of the California summer. In September, my youngest child would be leaving for college, U. C. Santa Barbara, and I figured the physical labor would be a perfect answer to ward off loneliness.

I don't know why this job turned out the way it did. I don't know if it was because my children were gone, or because I was feeling the first symptoms of menopause, or because it was the most physical of the jobs we'd undertaken. The explanation I lean towards has more to do with Pat's appearance on those fall days in the hills.

She wore leather gloves, a flannel shirt, blue jeans, and boots. After slicing through the trunk of a tree a few times, sweat stood on her brow. And she got dirty, we both did. To this day, if I see a woman in jeans and a flannel shirt, my heart leaps.

We'd come home exhausted, our truck weighted down with wood. Then we'd spend the weekend splitting the logs, then stacking the wood in Pat's back yard. Gradually, I started getting used to the physical labor, and liking the feel of my muscles being challenged.

We were actually making money this time. How could we not, with such low overhead? After a particularly hard day, Pat and I would sometimes soak in my spa, letting the jets pound on our tired muscles. If it were after dark, we'd go in naked.

It was on such a night that we first began playing with each other. She'd tease my pubic hair with her toes. I'd clench her nipples in mine. Like children playing in a bath, we thought, we were just being silly.

But I remember one day, a chilly day in November, when Pat ran her chain saw through a tree trunk and I stood transfixed, admiring her, and thinking how I wanted to get her home and into that spa.

That night when her foot went creeping up my thigh, I didn't push her away as I usually did. I spread my legs apart. I felt her foot press against my pubic bone, her heel against my clitoris. The last time I saw her face, lit by a distant street lamp, she was smirking.

She put her big toe inside me, and then she bent her knee and came closer. I don't know who started it, but we kissed, and then retreated to the house to make love. That night released a monstrous passion in me. Pat and I became ardent lovers.

It lasted two months, November and December. Then her husband caught us. He told my husband. They made us swear not to see each other again. But I was in no mood to obey my husband. I begged Pat to continue our affair, but she said her marriage was more important. It was just sex, after all, she said.

It wasn't just sex for me. I was in love with Pat. I suffered the loss of her with physical and emotional trauma. My husband left me because I couldn't stop loving Pat.

Pat and I have seen each other since, in safe surroundings, and she's been sympathetic, but she's adamant in her refusal to continue our affair. She's at least admitted to me that sex with me was always better than sex with her husband. It was the sex, the delicious, ecstatic sex that she remembered with longing.

Sometimes I wonder if things wouldn't have been better had Pat and I never known one another. Things would definitely be more comfortable. Perhaps some day when I'm over this I'll feel more sweet than bitter in remembering our affair. Now, I can't stop longing for her. In my fantasies, Pat is always wearing a red flannel shirt and blue jeans, a shock of her dark hair pasted to her sweaty brow. And I hear the whirr of a chain saw.

4

Just Experimenting…Not

It started with fantasies, deliciously erotic dreams about women I knew, at work, or strangers, but quite often Oprah. There's just something about her mouth.

What harm would it do, I told myself, to try it just once. (Did you ever hear of Lay's potato chips?)

I was happy as a straight woman, but sometimes you get a little bored, a little curious. I wanted to taste the forbidden fruit.

I promised myself not to become emotionally involved. Now, three years later, we're happily coupled and raising cockapoos.

*   *   *

This is the category for women who persuaded themselves that their interest in lesbian relationships was a sort of sexual liberalism. Essentially heterosexual, they were intrigued by the exotic.

Unlike the women who succumbed to an unexpected erotic attraction to a friend, these women acted with more conscious determination, sometimes pursuing the lesbian experience.

Although many women have homosexual encounters and remain primarily heterosexual, for these women, their first female lover became a revelation. What began as an adventure eventually became a way of life.

Jolene's Story

She was young and beautiful, and her skin was so soft. It was one of those really great moments in your life when you think to yourself, how come I never did this before.

When I called my sister for our routine weekly interstate chat, I happened to mention that I had a new good friend in California who was a lesbian.

"A real lesbian?" she asked.

"Yeah, a real lesbian. She's got a girlfriend and everything."

I think we both thought it was pretty cool. Coming from a small town in Utah to a big California city was quite a move for me. In general, I was unhappy with the change, but had to follow my job, and was happy enough to get out of the town where my ex-husband still kept coming around knocking on my door.

I'd met this lesbian friend of mine at work. Her name was Iris. She was a receiving inspector on the receiving line where I logged in trucks. We hit it off great and she helped me a lot on the job, trying to fit in. This was when you were hearing about lesbians everywhere you turned, and Ellen was about to come out on TV, and gay rights issues were in the news all the time.

I had never given any of it much thought before. But California was a new kind of life for me and my kids, and with the move came some new ideas. The more I hung out with Iris, the more interested I got in lesbian sex. She wasn't the least bit shy about answering my questions, so I asked.

Before my divorce, I had basically had sex with three men in my life, one being my jerk of a husband. One thing moving away did for me was to give me some freedom. Nobody in the new place knew me. At home, if I went out for pizza, my mom, dad, sister, and ex all knew about it the next day.

Even if the new job was boring, the new environment was not. It was about this time that I got my computer and started spending a lot of time online. I spent a lot of money buying things on the Internet, and I also ended up screwing around in chat rooms. There are some real weirdos on there. But also just some people looking for fun. I became more and more curious about sex with a woman, the more I learned about it. Also, the more I learned about it, and the more I recognized that lesbians were all around me, the more possible it seemed that it could come true.

Naturally, Iris was the first woman I asked to show me the ropes. I felt comfortable with her. She refused. She had a girlfriend, and maybe she wasn't attracted to me. I don't know. Maybe she thought I was just trouble, and maybe she was right. She suggested I put a personal ad on the lesbian bulletin board online. She helped me write it. Several women answered. Very frightening. We e-mailed each other and chatted online. Iris reviewed my e-mails to give me the benefit of her experience and authority, and I think she got off on the whole thing herself, imagining what it would be like for me to have my first time with a woman. She was treating it as if I was looking for a relationship, though, when all I really wanted was a walk on the wild side.

I wasn't quite bold enough, though, to accept the propositions coming my way. I opted instead for a threesome with a married couple. It was an exciting and frightening night. The man fucked his wife in front of me, and then he watched while she went down on me. I forgot he was there though after a few minutes and just let her lick me. She was young and beautiful, and her skin was so soft. It was one of those really great moments in your life when you think to yourself, how come I never did this before. Because it wasn't that strange, and it felt really good.

Of course, Monday morning I had to tell Iris all about it, and she was all smiles. She asked if I would see them again, and I wasn't sure. I thought that maybe I would, or maybe I would go back to one of those women who had answered my personal ad, now that I knew a little more, and I wasn't quite so afraid. So I tried it a couple more times before I managed to get transferred back home.

The odd thing was that when I went back to my small town in Utah, I discovered that there were lesbians there too. They had been there all along, but I had never noticed. That's good to know because I would hate to have to give up this new source of pleasure. I am not done with women by any means.

Samantha's Story

I liked knowing that she was attracted to me, and toyed with the idea of sleeping with her. I was bored with men, even gay men. This was something different.

I was forty-three and divorced with a long line of failed relationships littering my past. I'd lived with a couple of men, tried marriage for a few years, and had dated too many men to count. My best friend Ann was a happily married mother of two teenagers. On weekends we'd often pal around together, going to a movie or lecture or whatever. Since Ann's husband worked nights, her evenings were free to hang around with me.

One night we were talking about my attraction to gay men, which Ann didn't find as peculiar as I did. I'd even had a brief affair with a gay man. Ann thought it had something to do with their sensitivity. I thought it had something to do with their physical features, citing a typically smooth-faced, clean-chested look that turned me on. Nothing turned me off more than a hairy back, and though lots of gay men are hairy, there's a certain type, the effeminate ones, I suppose, that had always interested me.

"Why don't we go to a gay bar and watch the boys?" I suggested.

Ann was usually as ready for a lark as I was, so she agreed. I picked up a gay newspaper and hunted down the bars. We settled on the Pink Panther in a neighboring town. Ann and I started going there on Friday nights, sort of regularly, sitting at a table sipping fruity drinks and watching the hard-muscled young men dance together. At first I didn't pay much attention to the women.

Since I was with Ann, and presumably coupled, I felt pretty secure in my voyeurism. After about a month, some of the patrons and the male and female bartenders knew us by sight, if not by name.

One of the regulars, Candy, usually nodded towards us from her perch at the bar. She was a large woman, large in all ways, with a spiky gray hairdo. She wore Levis and drank Michelob. I noticed that when Ann went to the restroom, Candy caught my eye and smiled. One night she winked. I felt myself blush.

"Candy's flirting with me," I told Ann.

"Oh, yeah. Should I leave?"

We laughed at the joke. The next time we came, Candy asked me to dance. Adopting a defiant air, I glanced at Ann, and then said, "Sure."

Candy took hold of my hand and led me to the dance floor, where about six other couples, four female, danced to a romantic ballad I didn't know. Candy put her other hand on the small of my back. Obviously, she was going to lead. As we danced, I caught Ann's eye a couple of times. She raised her glass in a toast to my boldness.

"Why are you never here on ladies' night?" Candy asked me.

"What night is that?"

"Tuesday."

"I'm a working woman. I don't get out much on Tuesdays."

As a dancing partner, Candy was gallant and graceful. She stood at least a head taller than me, so I'm sure we looked absurd, even forgetting that we were both women. She had a small tattoo on her neck, I observed, a bird of some sort.

My response to this event was to feel like a naughty child, thrilled with getting away with something. It was fun.

Shortly thereafter, Ann started to worry that someone she knew would see us at the club. She was also getting bored with it. So we went bowling instead.

But I wasn't bored with the Pink Panther, so I decided to show up as a solo act on Tuesday. No hard-bodied men in sight, just women, a couple dozen of them. Jill was tending bar as usual, and there sat Candy on her stool, drinking her Michelob, her jeans stretched taut over her muscular thighs.

I went up and sat next to her. She seemed surprised and pleased that I'd come.

"Where's your friend?" she asked, "Ann, right?"

"Home with her family," I answered.

Candy raised an eyebrow, taking in the meaning of this answer. I didn't tell Ann about my Tuesday nights. The secretiveness only added to the excitement. Candy and I got to know each other better. I liked knowing that she was attracted to me, and toyed with the idea of sleeping with her. I was bored with men, even gay men. This was something different.

I watched with growing interest the other women, how they touched each other, their mannerisms and clothing. When I saw two women kiss, I felt it deep inside.

I told Candy that I'd never had sex with a woman.

"Would you like to?" she asked nonchalantly.

I said yes, not sure that I did. Candy had a tiny house in an old, but quaint part of town. I was nervous as we went inside. She gave me a large brandy to calm me down. She lit a couple of candles, turned off the electric lights, turned on some female version of Johnny Mathis. She led me to her bed, removed my clothes. Then she removed her clothes and brought my hands to her heavy breasts.

Then she made love to me. I say it that way because I was sort of passive that night, letting this thing be done to me. Candy moved on me methodically, in a scripted way, recognizing her role as teacher.

I liked it. I loved the kissing, the soft, sensuous kissing, full-lipped and luxurious. And the way her clever tongue lifted me to orgasm several times left me floating on a high for three days afterwards.

I thought I was just having fun, exploring an alternative means of pleasure. It was like that at first, with Candy. We spent a lot of nights together, and she taught me how to make love with a woman.

That was three years ago. I haven't been with a man since. After Candy and I stopped sleeping together, both because we were basically just friends and because she met someone else, I set out looking for a soul mate. A year later I found her. We're now a happy couple with a house and garden and an eight year old son. I've never felt so happy or at ease in my life. I feel like I've finally come home after years of nomadic wandering.

Mary's Story

After that night, we became a threesome, and I came to know the kiss of a woman's lips and the touch of her breast.

A strange set of circumstances led to my lesbianism. At forty-four, I divorced my husband and, practically destitute, moved in with my friend Joyce. It wasn't the best arrangement, but I couldn't afford my own place, not then. For the first few months, we got along fairly well. I landed a bookkeeping job and was beginning to feel that there was life after divorce after all. But then Joyce started seeing Max, and when he started sleeping over, I felt really out of place.

Sometimes I could hear them having sex, which was more than disturbing, but at midnight, where could I go? In addition to being disturbing, it could also be quite a turn-on, like watching a porno movie. I was going around all keyed up, exhausted from lack of sleep, and frantically counting my pennies in anticipation of the day I could move out.

One day Joyce asked me if I could hear them. "Max wants to know," she said.

"Sometimes," I said. "Why does he want to know?"

"It gives him a thrill."

"At my expense."

Joyce seemed embarrassed. We didn't ordinarily discuss sex, not even in the abstract. "Does it," she asked, staring at the table, "does it excite you?"

He's put her up to this, I knew. Sleazeball, I thought.

"Joyce, what's the point?"

"Well, he thinks you're sexy. He likes to think of you listening and being turned on. It's sort of become an obsession for him, actually. To tell you the truth, Mary, I'm beginning to get jealous."

Max was thirty-five, almost ten years younger than me, and good looking. I was both disgusted and flattered that he was interested.

"It's not very considerate of him to tell you," I said, disappointed with Joyce's characteristic lack of self respect.

"I know. Mary, he has this fantasy. He wanted me to ask you. I told him you'd refuse, but he begged me to ask you."

"What?"

"He wants to be with both of us. At the same time."

Now I was really disgusted. "Does he have two dicks?"

"Sorry. I promised I'd ask."

The subject wasn't mentioned again. I had a hard time looking Max in the eye after that. I tried to stay out of sight. But he knew I was there, and I knew he knew. Then they started leaving the bedroom door open. He was trying to lure me in. I lay in my room, my door open too, listening, masturbating. Incredibly, I began to look forward to this odd arrangement, pouring myself a cognac after they'd gone into the bedroom, and lying on my bed in a peignoir, without underwear. I'd sip my cognac, listening to the two of them wrestle each other to climax. Usually they did it twice.

One night I lay there, my fingers inside myself, after they had gone silent, clutching my breast with the other hand, when suddenly I saw Max standing in the dark beside the bed, naked and erect. He crawled on top of me. I moved my hand away and let him slide inside me. "Isn't this better?" he asked.

After that night, we became a threesome, and I came to know the kiss of a woman's lips and the touch of her breast. The first time we were together, Max fucked me doggie style, with Joyce underneath me, sucking my breasts. When Max pulled away, I lowered myself to Joyce, rubbing against her until I came. It wasn't long before I wanted Joyce to make love to me instead of Max, and I avoided intercourse with him. When he wasn't there, Joyce and I started having sex without him.

Eventually I no longer joined them when he came over. I wanted to be with Joyce, just the two of us, and relished those opportunities. Joyce kept referring to our lovemaking as "making do," as though it were second rate, a substitute for the real thing. I didn't see it that way. To me, making love to Joyce was wonderful, more wonderful than any sex I'd ever had.

When Max found out what was going on while he was away, he had a fit. It was okay if he were there, but the two of us together otherwise wasn't "right," in his peculiar style of morality. He accused Joyce of being a lesbian, a label she was unprepared to accept, and he forbade our relations. Unfortunately, Joyce has never been very strong willed. Despite my arguments, she was unable to disobey Max, and probably was more afraid of being a lesbian than anything else. As long as she'd been able to think of it as "making do," it was okay, but she couldn't think of it that way anymore.

Financially stable by then, I moved out, brokenhearted. But after a few years I look back on that time in a sort of disbelief. It was very strange and dreamlike. I don't think I was really in love with Joyce. I was just overcome by the joy of being with a woman. I've been with a couple others since then, and am learning what it means to be a lesbian. Unlike Joyce, I'm not afraid of that label. Quite the opposite. I cherish it and revel in it, and wish I'd embraced it sooner.

Petra's Story

After my orgasm (virtual, not actual), I had a choice of several things I could do to Mona. I chose to go down on her.

I don't know when exactly it started, my interest in women, but throughout the eighties, I read several novels featuring lesbians, including *Rubyfruit Jungle, Fried Green Tomatoes,* and *The Color Purple.* None of my female friends thought it odd that I was intrigued with the idea of a female lover. They were too, but none of us would ever go so far as to actually do it.

All along this was just a vague fantasy of mine which I never expected to act on. But then I discovered *Mona's Passion,* an interactive computer game which I downloaded from a bulletin board. The sysop had written the comment, "Must try—hot!" so of course everybody downloaded it. I had no idea what it was until I typed the word "PASSION" and the program went into action.

It asked me my name and my gender. Then it asked me who I wanted to take on my adventure, Mona (a buxom blonde) or Jerry (a fine-tuned hunk). I put aside my political conscience in favor of titillation and chose Jerry. The premise was that you were a detective trying to solve a murder mystery and Jerry (or Mona) was a tight-lipped key witness you had to extract clues from. The first time through the game, Jerry "probed my depths" with his "huge, hot penis," blurting out clues as we went along.

This is disgusting, I told myself. Then I played again, this time entering my gender as male and choosing Mona as my adversary. When she took my "trembling member into her hungry mouth," I slid further down in my desk chair. I got to poke her, front, back, and on the bathroom floor until she screamed out the name of the murderer.

Then I had a brainstorm. Was it possible that the sick creator of this game had been really imaginative? The third time through (by which time I was already limp with arousal), I entered my gender as female and chose Mona as my victim. The program didn't balk. My hands trembled at the hope that it was this sophisticated.

There she was, that simulated woman, nude in her shower. She saw me. She asked for a towel and I handed her one. She dried herself off and led me to the bedroom. She told me to take off my dress. Oh, what a clever programmer, I thought. Mona knows she's dealing with a woman. She kissed me. She touched my breasts. She squeezed the nipples. "I won't talk," she said. "No matter what you do to me. No matter how hard you beat me or how high you send me. Oh, God, Petra, you're so sexy."

To win the game, you collect all the clues, and to collect them, you ask for them at strategic moments. I didn't ask for any. I just kept torturing poor Mona. Did a man write this program? I wondered, melting in my chair as Mona "runs the tip of her tongue around the opening of your vagina. She takes your clit between her lips and pulls gently, then teases it with her tongue."

After my orgasm (virtual, not actual), I had a choice of several things I could do to Mona. I chose to go down on her. "Mona moans loudly as your tongue slides into her pussy. She's wet and anxious. Your nose is in her muff. You can smell the musky scent of her. You lick her eagerly, drinking in her juices. She goes wild, her hips moving. You hold her tightly on the bed, keeping your tongue on the spot while she bucks."

Mona and I did it every way the genius who wrote this program had imagined. There were lots of scenarios, lots of possible positions and accessories. This went on over a period of a couple weeks. Each time I got really turned on, I had to stop and finish myself off. I must have played this game dozens of times after that first day, ignoring the Jerry character altogether. I have to try this for real, I thought, and satisfy my curiosity once and for all. Virtual sex was interesting, but never will replace the real thing. I went in search of a flesh and blood Mona. When I found Katie, I told her that I was just curious, that I was a heterosexual and wasn't looking for a relationship. She was between lovers and was willing to have a diversion.

An experienced lesbian, Katie knew exactly how to make love to me. Technically, she was as good as Mona, but holding her real body in my arms was so much more wonderful. Katie was thorough and sensitive. No man had ever given me the kind of satisfaction she did, every time. Why would I go back to men, I asked myself, when this was so beautiful and natural? It wasn't just the sex, either. There was a compassion and intimacy between us, an instinctive understanding. I felt totally trusting with her. And we weren't even in love!

Now I'm looking for a woman to love, a permanent partner to spend the rest of my life with. I feel confident that this relationship, when it happens, will be better in all ways than any of my straight ones. I never made a very good heterosexual. Katie and I still see each other on occasion. She's my only sexual outlet for now. Well, unless you count Mona, of course.

5

I Always Knew, Sort of

I saw a bumper sticker which read, "Don't Die Wondering," and decided not to.

I've never been truly intimate with a woman, yet, in my heart, I know what I am. As I got older I thought there was something wrong with me, but that these "funny feelings" were just a stage I was going through.

I guess I had waited so many years for that kind of a relationship I was willing to take whatever came along.

All the signs were there, but I was too busy proving that I wasn't a lesbian to do anything other than get married and have children.

When my husband and I watched porno films, it was the female bodies that turned me on.

*   *   *

A large number of the respondents fell into this category. They described their suspicions about themselves with clues from their past: lack of interest in men, failure to fall in love with a man, intense relationships with women, sometimes recognizable physical attraction to female friends.

In some cases, an adolescent attraction to girls was forcibly suppressed, only to resurface much later. In other cases, the sexual interest in women developed gradually over time, becoming more and more focused. Many of these women didn't suspect that their intense friendships with women had any sexual root, and many also didn't realize that other women didn't have the same physical attraction to women they did. They thought it was "normal" to feel a desire for physical intimacy with close friends, an intimacy often manifested as innocent touching and hugging.

Some of these women suspected that they were lesbians from an early age, but thought they could outgrow the tendency or learn how to desire men. One woman married with the intention of "learning to love my husband." She didn't. Some did, however, love their husbands, but usually not with a sexual passion. Curiously, most of those who married were faithful wives and remained married for twenty or more years, remained married until they had their first female lover. In one sense, they can be said to have had "successful" marriages. Looking back now, they point to evidence all along that should have made a significant impression. Most common among the clues were excessive tomboyishness, crushes on women, heavy petting or sexual activity with other girls, no interest in men as sexual partners, lack of enjoyment of sex with men, lustful thoughts about other women, intense, obsessive friendships with women, lack of intimacy with a husband or male lover, intrigue about lesbians, desire to know lesbians, choosing an inordinate number of books and movies featuring lesbians, and fantasizing about sex with women.

If a woman had experienced many of these phenomena, some of us might want to ask, "But how could you not know?" The brain is a fascinating organ. One woman who could say "uh, huh" to almost all of the listed clues, put it charmingly: "And I still didn't figure it out."

She, and the others who contacted me, eventually did figure it out. These are some of their stories.

Barbara's Story

I kept pushing these feelings aside, not willing to live a homosexual lifestyle, not willing to admit it, even to myself.

In retrospect, I probably suspected that I was gay at the age of sixteen when I had a crush on an older woman. Because I was so insecure and naive about sex, I didn't even consider taking the relationship further than a friendship. The woman was very kind, supportive, and loving to that young teenager. So my first response was to suppress the urge, not risk rejection, and settle for a warm friendship.

Later, in my early twenties, I became attracted to a woman my own age. I was certain that she was gay. She was in a relationship with another woman. I wasn't yet sure enough to express my feelings, especially as I didn't want to risk rejection.

I didn't have sex with a man until I was twenty-nine, so I guess I was a "late bloomer" all around. I was never tempted to marry, and continued feeling vague urges towards women. I kept pushing these feelings aside, not willing to live a homosexual lifestyle, not willing to admit it, even to myself.

At age forty, I finally entered a relationship with a woman. This is the greatest relationship I've ever had. I'm for the first time willing to be open with all my close friends, all of whom have been very accepting and supportive. I've had the pleasure of coming out to those I've wanted to know, and am willing to discuss my sexuality with those who inquire.

I've been with my partner two years, and we're going strong. We held a wedding ceremony and consider ourselves married. One of these days my mother will make inquiries. I'll be open to discussion. Like those friends that I've been open with, I suspect that my mother will regret that she wasn't invited to witness our wedding ceremony, at least I hope so.

Because my lover has been an active member of the local gay community, I am now part of the community too, and I love it.

Bridget's Story

I had begun to understand who I was, what I was. I was overjoyed with this new understanding.

My decision to become a nun had more to do with a fear of marriage than with religious fervor, but at the time, I believed my reasons were honorable. I had never been interested in men, had never wanted a boyfriend, had never wanted to have children.

In my day, and with my upbringing, there were very few choices for a young woman. Usually, you got married. Being a Catholic, I had this other option.

I remember visiting an Amish village in Pennsylvania and learning that Amish women marry and have twelve children. The only women who don't are the ones who, by virtue of their academic excellence, become the teachers, and the teachers are not allowed to marry. That made me think of teachers as some higher form of life.

So I became a nun and a teacher. Among the sisters, I knew of a few of what we called "special friendships." They were officially discouraged, but as long as they didn't interfere with work, nobody cared that much, really. Over the years, I often wondered about those special friendships and what those sisters did together. I was curious, but I refrained from participation, and I counseled more than one of these women on the wickedness of fleshly delights.

I sort of believe that nunneries have traditionally been a refuge for lesbians. In earlier times, women who didn't want marriage had very few options. I believe now that I was such a woman. These days, women have so many more options, and some women did then, too, but I didn't know much about that.

Living in a community of women appealed to me. As I got older, I assumed a sort of protective, maternal role over the initiates, officially and unofficially. In recent times, many of these women aren't the traditional eighteen year old virgins. They're older, more experienced women.

One of these was Dolores, a thirty-eight year old Latin beauty with blue-black hair and huge brown eyes. I think I fell in love with her the moment we met. Dear God, what havoc she caused in my heart. After all those years, at forty-one, my resolve was broken. I prayed for strength. I prayed for Dolores to disappear. I prayed for myself to disappear. But there she was, day after day, looking forlornly up at me with those adoring, respectful eyes. I always felt like she was flirting with me. I had begun to think that I was going to have to kill myself. But that's sort of a worse sin than oral sex, isn't it?

Well, once she understood what I wanted, we spent some sinfully passionate hours together. She seemed to have no moral qualms about it, but I was still tormented. Despite my attempts to hide my love for Dolores, we were found out. I was reprimanded. But I couldn't control myself. I had begun to understand who I was, what I was. And after a time I was overjoyed with this new understanding. If it conflicted with my calling, then my calling must be wrong, not my blossoming identity.

I left the order. I never left God, though. I don't believe that God would condemn love between two people, and I regret my earlier support of a system that does so. I believe that the Church is evolving, but it's moving too slowly for me. Service to the Lord may once have been a way out for lesbians, but we no longer have to compromise our spiritual beliefs to conform to the only safe haven.

Lynn's Story

I always had a best friend or two, was always closer in my friendships than my friends were used to.

I guess I've known all my life that my feelings about women were . . . unusual? Teenage crushes on teachers and camp counselors, I passed off as a phase. My dearest high school friend and I snuggled together in bed on our weekend overnights and petted each other.

"Do you think we're lesbians?" I asked her more than once.

Her answer was firmly negative.

Wanting nothing more than to have children, be taken care of, and fit the norm, I married and had three children and a decent, but distant, marriage. Doubts haunted me for years. Fantasies too. I suffered tremendous fear and guilt, though I never acted on my feelings. I always had a best friend or two, was always closer in my friendships than my friends were used to.

At forty-two, with a less than satisfying marriage, I openly confronted my feelings towards other women, and began to explore them, discussing them with people I trusted. Then I met her, a much younger woman of twenty-five, straight, with whom the connection was undeniably deep. We came together like magnets.

The energy was incredible and frightening. My relationship with this passionate young woman opened and released me into my fully loving nature. She was clearly overwhelmed by it all, and within a few months, it was over. But that was just the beginning for me. Soon after that the true love of my life arrived. I left my husband of nearly twenty-five years. I've been with my partner twelve years. Our life has been incredibly blessed. My adult children love her to pieces.

I've pondered deeply my lifestyle and my "orientation." Sexuality has never been the overriding issue, but the depth of the relationship and the levels of honest exploration have been more important. At last I feel that my personal growth is moving in the right direction.

Dorothy's Story

Throughout these years, I never understood that I actually was a lesbian. Instead, I called myself, "a woman who happens to be in love with another woman."

I spent so much of my early life worrying that I might be a lesbian, that it amazes me now, at 48, to realize how long I actually waited.

The first time I seriously considered that I might be a lesbian was when I was 16. My best friend Cindy and I wondered if the way we felt about each other was "natural" or not. We approached my mom and asked her if she thought we were lesbians. Mom assured me that we weren't, and, relieved, we resumed our plans for a future together. Our plans included that we would each get married and that our husbands would then get killed in some sort of tragic accident leaving us happily widowed together.

When I was 19 I met my first real-life lesbian, and fell madly in love with her. She was already in a committed relationship, and I knew there was no way I could compete with the powerful, intelligent, accomplished woman who was her lover. Instead, I vowed to love Barbara all my life, and then followed the man I was dating to Hawaii. A year later, in a letter to Barbara, I told her I was going to marry the man. This short announcement was followed by a passionate three page torrent of words about how wonderful I believed lesbian relationships were and how much I wished I were a lesbian. It's hard to remember, but I seemed to feel some sort of obligation to be heterosexual if I could possibly stand it. I believe my criteria was throwing up. I thought that as long as I could have sex with a man and not throw up, then I must be straight. I sure did long to be a lesbian, though.

I struggled with this over the next twenty years or so, with intermittent borderline lesbian episodes. I remember watching *Personal Best* over and over one month on HBO. That was before the days of VCRs, and I figured out all the times it would show and made sure that I was alone in the living room, watching it. I remember meeting another lesbian, my second one after Barbara, and making out with her one evening. Her name was Alice and she was a striking, six-foot tall blonde amazon. She and I were graduate students together and she confessed to me one evening that she was a lesbian. Within a week I was sitting on her lap and we were passionately kissing, only to be interrupted by the return of my roommate. We both scrambled to our feet, and the next day, Alice was very uncomfortable around me, and we never spoke in private again. I think that what confused her was that by this time in my life, I was married to my third husband, and so she saw me as straight (as did I, of course). However, what I was living was the perfect life for a lesbian who didn't know it yet, with him in Missouri and me in Oklahoma.

There was one more incident, another drunken evening with another student, a straight one this time who was "just experimenting." Throughout all those years, though, my heart and my loyalty remained with Barbara, my first and only true love. I honestly believed that by sleeping only with men and not with women, I was remaining true to her. Every time I got involved with a man I told him about Barbara up front. I always said the same thing, that she was my true love and that if she ever would have me as her lover, I would leave him and go to her. If the man was willing to be in a relationship with me under those circumstances, then I was comfortable knowing I was not deceiving him.

Throughout these years, I never understood that I actually was a lesbian. Instead, I called myself, "a woman who happens to be in love with another woman." And of course, I never really expected anything to come of it, still seeing Barbara as unreachable and beyond my dreams. Then, one day, when I was 42, I got a phone call from her. Her lover had left her, her job was in ruins, her life was a mess. Could I come out for a visit? I got the first plane I could out to her place. Barbara lived in the country outside a small town, and it took several hours to get there. She met me at the airport, and as we drove she talked, telling me everything about her life these past few years, her dashed dreams, her disappointments. She told me about a number of men she had been with (for she did not, at this time, identify herself as a lesbian, either. Rather, she considered herself a woman without bias, be it racial or gender). In the course of talking about men, she said, 'I'll never sleep with another married man again."

"And does that apply to married women, as well?" I asked her, not daring to look her in the face. That question changed it all, and within weeks, we were lovers.

I've been a lesbian now for six years. Barbara and I, predictably, are no longer together. After waiting for her for over 20 years, I discovered we were just too different to be a couple, after all. But I have discovered the joy of lesbianism, of community, of coming home. I've marched in Gay Pride parades, I've gone to countless potlucks, and I'm in a wonderful relationship with a woman I love very much. I can't explain why I felt like I had some sort of obligation to society to be heterosexual, but at least I can say I gave it a good, honest try. I don't really regret the years that I spent with my husbands and male lovers. That's a valuable part of my life and it is all part of who I am and what my destiny is turning out to be. But for now, and for the rest of my life, I'm very happy and relieved to have been true to myself at last.

Leila's Story

There were times I thought what a loss it was that there was nothing we could do as two women to express our feelings, nothing sexual.

As a child, I had crushes on several grown women—teachers and friends of the family. My first memory of a powerful attraction to another girl was when I was fourteen. We were in the same gym class. I fell in love with her. Nothing came of it, but I remember the feeling. A year or two later, a girlfriend and I played at falling into each other's arms, literally, then lying there on the floor for a few moments. When I was seventeen and eighteen, I snuggled with girlfriends a few times at pajama parties. It was a thrill that I remember even now, half a century later.

When I was twenty-two, I fell in love with a woman. I didn't call it that at the time, didn't think of it that way, but our friendship continued. There were times I thought what a loss it was that there was nothing we could do as two women to express our feelings, nothing sexual.

This was in the forties and I'd never heard of lesbians and lacked the imagination or the courage to explore, although Jane might have been open to it then. Some years later, she was staying with me and we shared a bed. She touched me in the night on my buttocks and thighs. I pretended to sleep, but I was thrilled by the feeling. My love for her and my intense attraction continued (in spite of her first three marriages) for another forty years.

I was in my early thirties, living in Paris, before I was aware of knowing any lesbians. When a friend came out to me, I was both fascinated and terrified. Later, after she had broken up with her lover and was visiting, she made love to me. I was drunk at the time and probably scared, but later I couldn't stop thinking about her, wanting to be lovers. She decided she'd rather be friends than lovers, and couldn't see that we could be both.

While I was a drinking alcoholic, I did have sex with several women. By then, I had figured out what two women could do. At the same time, I was still sleeping with men, which was never as satisfying in any way, but I was attracted to some of them. By then, the late sixties, I never had sex without alcohol, and usually I would actually be drunk. On New Year's Eve, 1970, at forty-seven, I had my last drink, my last drunk, and that was the last time I had sex with a man.

With recovery and sobriety, I made profound changes in my life. That first sober year, I was in a warm, supportive relationship with another woman, a dear friend. This was in New York City in the early days of women's and gay liberation. Mary was active in women's lib, a new world to me. I became an activist too. My circle of friends shifted from mostly heterosexual couples to women, mostly lesbians. In 1973, I had been two and a half years sober, two and half years with women only. I was with a lover who was a militant in gay liberation. A gay civil rights ordinance was being introduced at the city council, and hundreds of gays and lesbians gathered outside City Hall to lobby for passing it. We stood for hours in cold rain with our placards and our chants while the straight men inside debated and eventually voted against the ordinance. That was my first real coming out, in front of TV cameras, the first time I really called myself a lesbian. It was exhilarating gathering with so many excited and angry gay men and lesbians. I had found and claimed my new world at age fifty.

I believe that for me becoming a lesbian was a choice. It wasn't a choice I could have made earlier because I hadn't even seen it as a possibility, it was so deeply hidden in the silence of this culture. And it may not have been a choice I could have made at another time in another place. It was easy coming out in that burst of women's and gay liberation in a city of eight million people, and I'm grateful I was then and there.

Gina's Story

We exchanged small talk. I kept thinking, "A lesbian is talking to me." I was thrilled.

It took me forty years to finally quit lying to myself. I kept denying it, kept trying to change it. And by the time I knew it could no longer be denied, I still was afraid to act on the knowledge. Finally, as Nike advises, I decided to just do it.

Once I make a decision, I don't falter much. I was going to get laid, pure and simple. Last year my friend Mary, a lesbian, had plans to go to the West Coast Women's Festival in the Sierra Nevada mountains over Labor Day weekend. It was a lesbian haven where Mary thought a person might be able to get laid if she worked at it. Mary and her lover offered to give me a ride.

The festival lasts four days and three nights, plenty of time, I thought. We arrived at the remote campground Thursday afternoon. I pitched my little tent under a tree, and then went off exploring a phenomenon I could never have imagined. There were thousands of them, thousands of women letting it all hang out, literally. I stared. A few women were completely naked. Several were topless. All sizes, shapes, and colors of breasts paraded by. I tried to look cool, examining the crafts, reading the bulletin board, and listening to the music. I watched the CW dancing lessons, regretting my single status. I watched volleyball, a soccer match, and sat in on a workshop on Wicca.

Everyone was friendly and warm. But when someone smiled at me or spoke to me, I got very nervous. Several times that first evening I wished I'd never come. I decided to forget about getting laid. I'd just try to absorb some of the culture. I hung out with Mary during the evening performances and went to my tent to sleep about one in the morning.

Friday after breakfast I bought some earrings from an artist with huge breasts and a blue and green hairdo. Then I sat on a log to hear the music at the day stage—a trio singing original compositions. A comic appeared next, most of her jokes sexually explicit. She did a bit about alternative types of dildos, alternative to the traditional phallus style. It was pretty funny.

As I was laughing at this skit, a woman sat next to me. I glanced to see who it was. She smiled. I smiled. She was about my age, thin, wearing dark sunglasses, a T-shirt, and khaki shorts.

"Hi," she said.

"Hi," I said.

"Is she any good?"

I nodded. We listened to the rest of the performance. Before the next performer, the woman beside me introduced herself. Her name was Toby. She was from Sacramento and had been coming to this festival for four years. I told her it was my first time. We exchanged small talk. I kept thinking, "A lesbian is talking to me." I was thrilled. When a singer came on that I didn't care for, Toby asked if I'd had lunch. "Oh, God," I thought, "she wants to eat with me."

We had a hamburger, sitting on a patch of grass in the shade. We talked some more. Toby seemed intelligent. She listened well and seemed interested in my life, though there were several things I didn't tell her. I let her assume that I was a lesbian, I mean, already well entrenched. Toby was a substance abuse counselor and had a twelve year old daughter, the product of artificial insemination. We talked about her daughter.

Toby usually came to the festival with someone, but this year, although some of her friends were here, she was uncoupled. I told her I was in the same situation. There had been a joke about festival predators earlier that day, on stage, and I got the impression that there were a few women here whose goal was to make some quick conquests. I wondered if Toby was one of these.

When we sat down to eat, she took off her sunglasses, so I finally got to see her eyes. They were blue, edged by tiny lines which deepened when she smiled. I wondered if she was interested in me. I began to have renewed interest in my original plan. After sitting on the grass for an hour talking, we went to a workshop on lesbian motherhood. When Toby and I looked at each other, she smiled with a sort of curl to her lip. A suggestion, surely. What is she waiting for, I thought?

It was a hot afternoon, a fact that we'd commented on more than once.

"You know," Toby said, after the workshop ended, "I've got an ice chest full of Budweiser in my camper. Would you like one?"

I froze. What do I do, I wondered. Well, Gina, I told myself, you came here to get laid. It's possible this woman wants to oblige you. "It sounds like just the thing," I told her, freaking out on the inside.

We walked across a field to where her pickup and camper were parked. Inside she took two chilly bottles of beer from an ice chest. The camper was filled with a mattress. It was the only place to sit. We drank the cool brew and talked some more. After a while, Toby said, "Gina, I'd really like to kiss you." On the inside, I screamed in panic. On the outside, I said, "I'd like that."

Toby kissed me. She kissed me again. We kissed some more. Her lips seemed to fit into mine so easily, so perfectly. There was nothing odd about it. God, I thought, a lesbian is kissing me. We continued kissing for quite a while, lying side by side on the mattress.

When she unhooked my bra and touched my breast, I cried out involuntarily in fear. Toby pulled back, looking confused. She sat up, staring at me. Oh, shit, I thought, I've ruined it.

"Did I hurt you?" Toby asked.

"No. No, of course not."

After a brief silence, she said, "You've never done this, have you?"

I shook my head.

"Why didn't you tell me?" Toby asked. I remembered my first time with a man, when I was twenty-three. I had told him. I'd told him before it had happened, as he was removing my clothes. But he'd just laughed and said, "Oh, sure, right." And he'd fucked me without ceremony.

"Let's talk," Toby said. "Tell me your story, and this time tell me the truth." She gave me another beer. I told her about my straight life and how I'd come to recognize my lesbianism. I kept thinking that maybe she didn't want to make love to me if I hadn't done it before. And why would she? I wouldn't know what to do. I didn't tell Toby that I'd come here with the goal of getting laid, maybe because it had become personal now, and that sounded so stark. I liked her. I wanted her to kiss me again.

"Are you sure you want to be here?" Toby asked.

I nodded. I was getting more and more sure.

"Well, then," she said, "it will my pleasure to initiate you." She proceeded slowly, kissing everything as my clothes came off. She kissed my stomach and breasts, my neck and shoulders, even my arms. No one had ever kissed my arms, the biceps and the spot on the inside of the elbow. She licked me and sucked on my earlobes and nipples. It was sublime.

Toby pulled off her T-shirt, revealing her small firm breasts. She pressed herself against me, our breasts touching. I put my arms around her warm back. It felt so natural holding her.

"Are you okay?" she asked.

I nodded. "Lovely."

She pulled off my shorts, then slowly removed my panties, stroking my thighs and stomach as she went. Her fingers raked through my pubic hair, and then she was lying between my legs, her lips grazing my upper thigh. I could feel myself trembling with anticipation. Toby kissed me lightly all around the triangle, her face brushing against it. Then she parted the lips of my cunt with her fingers and pressed her tongue flat against me. She licked me, lightly, slowly, and kept the rhythm perfectly. I felt my tension subside as I gave myself over to her. There was nothing to be afraid of, I told myself. This was wonderful. I became more and more excited, until I couldn't stand it anymore. I was straining and moaning and wondered if she was ever going to let me go over the edge. Finally, she did, her tongue directly on target. I think I must have yelled rather loudly when I came. I had this horrifying image then of a hundred people crowded around the outside of the camper, like that scene on Star Trek where Captain Kirk is all alone on the Enterprise and opens one of the portals to see dozens of faces peering in at him.

Toby pulled herself up to face me. "Nicely done," she said, then kissed me deeply. I smelled and tasted my cunt on her mouth. I sucked her lower lip.

"That was incredible," I told her. "Nobody's ever done that to me before, I mean, not all the way to the end."

Straddling me, Toby wriggled into a position where our genitals touched. She pressed her face into my neck and moved her pelvis in a sort of slow gyration. "This one's for me," she whispered. "You move too, same rhythm, but opposite."

I tried to do as she asked, moving up and down against her, up when she came down. I knew when I got it right because she gasped. I didn't quite know what we were doing, but she seemed to like it. Toby's breathing became rough and erratic as she became more excited. Feeling her breath on my neck and our bodies touching like they were, I had a hard time remaining calm enough to do my part. But Toby came very quickly, leaving me highly aroused.

She moved to my side and reached a hand down to where the juices were flowing. Her tongue slid into my mouth as her fingers slid into my vagina. She pressed her palm against my pubic bone and pumped it, her fingers going in and out, until I climaxed again. When I'd caught my breath, I kissed her face and mouth and held her tightly. We lay very still on the mattress for at least half an hour. Then Toby suggested we go take a shower and eat dinner. If we waited much longer, there wouldn't be any food. I wasn't very hungry, just overwhelmed by this experience. I wanted more. I wanted to go down on her. But, I reasoned, she was probably ready to get rid of me, so I warned myself against becoming a nuisance to her.

I felt sort of delirious, but I followed along, showering in the communal shower and eating in the communal dining hall. I ran into Mary on the steps afterward. She asked me where I'd been all day. Just then Toby came out of the hall and stood beside me. Mary grinned. I introduced them. Mary kept grinning.

Toby saw someone she knew and excused herself. While she talked to her friend, Mary and I moved off. I wanted to spare Toby the trouble of trying to find a kind way to shake me. I told Mary what had happened and she congratulated me. We found seats for the evening show while I kept reviewing the afternoon in my mind. I looked for Toby in the crowd, but didn't see her. I hoped that at least I'd get a chance to thank her properly before the weekend was over.

At ten o' clock, during a break in the show, the emcee came on stage and said, "I have a plea from a desperate woman." She read the note in her hand. "Gina, you beautiful dyke, where the hell are you? I'm waiting by the ice wagon. Toby." Then the emcee laughed and said, "For Christ's sake, Gina, don't let this woman suffer any longer."

Mary nudged me. I was shocked. But I was out of my seat in a flash. I asked someone where the ice wagon was and rushed to it. Toby wants me, that's all I could think, and I was overjoyed.

We went back to her camper and made love. I went down on her this time. I was so happy to give her an orgasm that way. We made love throughout the night, and spent all day Saturday and Sunday morning together. It was very hard leaving Toby that Sunday. We exchanged phone numbers and addresses, and I've seen her since, but the distance between us makes a real relationship impossible.

That weekend is the best thing that ever happened to me. I'll cherish it for the rest of my life. And Toby will always be a dear friend. I love her and am so grateful to her. I know she's fed up with hearing me say "thank you." I can't help it. I spent half of my life miserable. I had never felt joy before I met her. I kick myself often for having waited so long, for being afraid.

Kay's Story

I never enjoyed sex with him, but it was a wife's duty, after all.

My guardian, whom I called "Mom," always accused me of being a lesbian. I felt it was because of her anger over her sister being one. In the fifties, this was a very taboo subject. Her sister was probably the person nicest to me in my childhood. Her partner was beautiful and kind. They weren't around very much, not often enough for me.

I was a tomboy who never played with dolls and spent most of my childhood working hard. I met my husband-to-be at thirteen. Mom picked him out and invited him to visit our home on an ongoing basis. We went together for eight years, never engaging in sex, just heavy petting. When he went into the service, I had no interest in dating other men. I joined the Navy Reserve and worked on a base with six hundred men and three women. The only one I cared to talk to was another woman. I enjoyed coffee with her and liked her a lot, but didn't think anything of this.

I became engaged to my boyfriend while he was in the service. After I joined, I got a "Dear Jane" letter from him. He broke up with me because I joined the service, and "only lesbians do that." My heart was broken.

A few months later my ex-boyfriend came home. The breakup didn't stick. We got married and had three children. I never enjoyed sex with him, but it was a wife's duty, after all. I continued to have stronger affections for women than men, but didn't associate this with lesbianism. I kept working. I've always worked hard.

When I was forty-eight, a lesbian friend asked me to intercede between herself and her girlfriend. They were fighting. I spent a lot of time on the phone with Ellie, who lived in another state. Next thing I knew, Ellie and I had become friends. We talked long distance almost every day for about nine months. When the two of them broke up, my friend told me she didn't want me to talk to Ellie anymore. I was devastated, and felt like I was losing the only real friend I ever had. I hadn't cried since I was nine, but when this happened, I broke down and couldn't stop.

I called Ellie and told her I thought I loved her. She invited me to visit. I flew down immediately. I knew we were in love. This was the first time I ever felt what love was. After this, I realized that what I felt for my husband was something else. He was my only childhood friend and my protector.

Unfortunately for me, Ellie had grabbed me on the rebound. We lasted only six months. She went on to fall in love several more times and is now planning to marry a man, her sixth husband.

The short, wonderful time I was in this relationship made me aware that I really loved being with a woman. I felt like I had come home and found my niche. It was extremely difficult to end my twenty-seven year marriage and tell my children. It's been three years now, and my husband will never recover. He has tried to commit suicide twice and has gone back to drinking after being dry for sixteen years. My children, on the other hand, are wonderful about it, and are very supportive of me.

I think I'm still in love with Ellie, but am trying to get over it so I can get on with my life and meet someone new. I realize how special that first woman is, especially if it happens so late in life.

6

Bowled Over by an Unexpected Lust

At the age of 42, I embarked on an affair with a woman and discovered that I had been sleeping with the wrong sex all these years.

I've never felt so out of control. I wanted her like it was coming out of the primitive core of my being.

I ached all over to take her to bed, but kept wondering what I would do with her if I did.

I was so horny by then, I could have gotten off on the side of an idling bus.

       *   *   *

For these women, it hit suddenly and powerfully. They had no inkling of their lesbian tendencies until they fell for another woman, wanted her without considering the ramifications of their desire. Usually, they didn't struggle with their new sexual identity because it was so overwhelming that they didn't need to ask questions. They slipped quite comfortably into the role of loving another woman. Once they recognized their feelings of lust, they pursued the cause of it, never looking back.

In most of these stories, the other woman was known to be a lesbian, which is probably significant. The narrator knew that at least the subject of her affection was predisposed to loving women. Knowing that, she might think of the lesbian as a potential lover. Once the possibility has been established, emotions can follow.

There's a self-protective reflex in most of us that prevents us from wanting something that's not available. This idea may have a relevance beyond this chapter. The availability of lesbian sex makes it much more likely that a woman would develop a desire for it.

Betty's Story

It wasn't long before I began to fantasize about sex with Chantra. I was baffled and overwhelmed by my desire.

My life was pretty routine until 1986 when I decided to go back to college and finish my Master's. My son was a teenager, my husband successfully settled in his career. Before this, I'd always thought it was just a joke about what happens to women who go back to school, about how they start thinking for themselves, broaden their horizons, lose respect for their husbands, want more out of life, fall for their professors.

But I wasn't a naive, dewy-eyed housewife who'd lived under the aegis of my husband and had never experienced the world. I was an educated, sophisticated woman who had consciously chosen to marry at twenty-four, who had consciously chosen to bear a child at twenty-six, and who had consciously chosen to resume my career in psychology at forty-one.

I didn't fall for my professor. I fell for a classmate, a sensationally bright, energetic, fascinating woman of thirty-six. Almost from the first class I was captivated by her. We joined forces for a research project and met outside class in the library and at coffee shops.

It wasn't long before I began to fantasize about sex with Chantra. I was baffled and overwhelmed by my desire. I didn't think much about what it meant, I mean, in the larger picture. I just knew I wanted her.

Two and half months into the semester, we met at her apartment to study, and I seduced her. She seemed happy about it at first, but I think guilt caught up with her, and our affair turned complicated. My marriage broke up over Chantra, but by then, we were no longer seeing each other.

In 1988, I had dinner with a woman I'd known for years, Teresa. We'd never been real friends, but I liked her, and I felt comfortable with her. During the course of our conversation, I told her about Chantra, an event which loomed out there like a billboard on my life's highway. Teresa told me she too was trying to recover from her first experience with a woman, and, just like me, wasn't sure what her next move would be. It seemed that we had been through the same wringer.

Not long after that evening, Teresa and I became lovers. I think we were both just trying it out, trying to see if we really did want another woman. Well, I guess we did. We've been together ever since. Teresa was wonderful with my son, and even managed to help bring my ex-husband to a point where we could all be friends. I think it's relieved the burden of guilt for him seeing that I'm really a lesbian after all and there wasn't much he could do about that.

With Teresa to help me, the transition into this new world has been very smooth for me. I'm happy with my life now, and am working in a program to provide vocational skills to women on welfare.

Rita's Story

We continued to rehearse being lovers on stage. By the time the play opened, I was in love with Maisie/Corinne. The first time I saw her in costume, my swoon was real.

It happened to me in 1988, a year I consider the beginning of a new life. Underappreciated on my job as a high school English teacher, I indulged myself in community events, especially theater, which I've always loved. Sometimes I volunteered to do sets, but when a part came along which interested me, I acted as well.

I was cast as Mona in a loose adaptation of the life of a Victorian era English poet, Maisie Crawford. In the play, Maisie fell for Mona and spent part of the time seducing her and part of the time fighting with her husband, all amid writing poetry.

Playing the part of Maisie was Corinne, a striking, intense woman who seemed born to the role. She was in her late forties, a lesbian, and an actress I'd admired for years. We knew each other only casually before that summer.

My boyfriend Ian choreographed the lighting for the play, so he was on hand at rehearsals. I knew that this play was going to be an event for me, but not quite in the way it was. There was one scene between Corinne and myself which presenting me with a true artistic challenge. We were to kiss, passionately, "with the hunger of a starving person," I was told. The other scenes between us were to be equally passionate, though not physical.

During rehearsals, there was a lot of joking around. Corinne seemed amused at my discomfort. "There's no fire between you," the director criticized. "I want fire. These women are crazed with lust." The first time we tried the kiss, I just couldn't bring myself to do it. As soon as Corinne leaned towards me, I'd bust up laughing.

"Look, Rita," the director said, "close your eyes and imagine yourself alone with Paul Newman. Or Clint Eastwood, or whoever turns you on." I tried. I closed my eyes and felt Corinne's arms around me. I thought of Don Johnson. I could see the crinkles around his eyes. I put my arms around Corinne and our mouths came together. It wasn't very convincing. "This is going to take practice," the director said. "The most important thing your character has to be is wanting Maisie, wanting her like an animal. That's essential. Rita, I want you to practice lust until we meet again Monday evening."

"Sorry," I told Corinne.

She laughed. "It's okay. You'll get it. I've seen you work before. You just have to get serious first, you know, get more involved. You're holding back."

How does one practice lust? I asked myself. Ian was overjoyed with my weekend assignment. We practiced lust together. He went so far as to wear one of my bras and put on a wig. I think he enjoyed that most of all.

During the next couple of weeks, I grew more fond of Corinne, watching her act, drawn in by the intensity of character that was partly Maisie, partly Corinne. We didn't rehearse the seduction scene again until the third week. By then, I felt more comfortable with Corinne and more involved in my role. Now when she turned her fiery gaze on me, I actually felt quivery.

"Last summer in the country," Maisie said, stepping towards me with a determined gaze, "when I saw you in that blazing white dress, I swore I'd have you, some day. I'd have you so welded to my soul that to separate us would mean mutual annihilation."

We fell into each other's arms. I felt myself go weak as she closed her mouth over mine. We kissed, long and deeply, in a frantic embrace. I held her, clutching her back, feeling like I was about to be swallowed, or drowned. As our mouths came apart, I heard myself sigh audibly. That's not in the script, I thought, alarmed.

Corinne and I stood with our arms still around each other, looking at each other. She looked positively bewildered. I turned to our director, who just stared. At last Corinne's arms fell away.

"Perfect!" yelled the director. "My God, that was perfect."

Later, Ian told me that he'd been really turned on by that kiss. So was I, I thought. So was Corinne, I discovered. After that, I knew that I was truly attracted to her, but I didn't know how much of it was just trying to be Mona, or how much of what I saw in her was the poet Maisie.

We continued to rehearse being lovers on stage. By the time the play opened, I was in love with Maisie/Corinne. The first time I saw her in costume, my swoon was real. She wore tan and cream, men's country dress, felt trousers, a white blouse with ruffles along the front and cuffs, a tightly-buttoned vest, and a cocked felt hat. She was stunning in that old-fashioned, fuzzy-lensed way that makes period pieces so attractive. I wore a sky-blue satin gown with puffed up sleeves and low-cut bodice, and a full hoop under the skirt. I have a photograph of the two of us embracing in those costumes, displayed prominently in my front room.

"Come home with me after the play," I asked her on opening night. She shook her head in dismay. "I can't, Rita. I have someone else to go home to." The yearning and passionate tension of my true life desire filled my acting with reality. The reviews were excellent. The usual faction was appalled. So much the better for the box office.

The play ran its intended three weeks, four performances each week. Twelve times I kissed Corinne in public, looked with longing into her face, tore myself from her arms in a heartbreaking farewell scene.

"It's the play," she told me when I begged her to make love to me. "You've gotten too wrapped up in the play."

"It's not just the play," I insisted. "I've never felt like this before. I've never wanted anything so much. I've never looked into someone's eyes and felt my knees give way."

After the play's run, I finally got Corinne into bed. It was wonderful. I'd known it would be. Why hadn't I done this before, I kept asking myself. I broke up with Ian. Corinne's lover didn't know about us, and Corinne suffered terrible guilt over her deception. We saw each other infrequently over a two-year period. In 1991, I met Rose, one of many lesbians Corinne introduced me to. This one took.

Anyone who witnessed my performance as Mona, including Ian, isn't much surprised about my new lifestyle. It was apparently a role I was born to play.

Kiri's Story

As she took another piece of lettuce into her mouth, I had a vivid image of those lips approaching mine, and for the first time in my life, I felt sexual desire for a woman.

Sometimes I think all this talk about past lives and time warps, or whatever, has some merit. I've had a few mysterious experiences in my life which suggest that our lives are more complex than we are generally aware.

One fall day in 1990 I sat at a steel table on an outside patio of a New York cafe, drinking a glass of chardonnay and reading *Millie's Book*. I've got to admit I wasn't able to concentrate well on the book and so noticed the people coming and going around me.

After about a half hour, a well-dressed woman was seated at another table. She ordered a diet cola and a Caesar salad. Her auburn hair was cut short, bobbed. She was tall and long-legged. After she was settled, I went back to my book.

When the waiter brought her cola, I looked up again. As the waiter left, the woman looked my way. I saw her face clearly. She looks terribly familiar, I thought. I searched my memory to pin some identity on her. I knew I'd seen her before. But more than familiarity struck me. As our eyes met, I felt some deep stirring of my being. Sometimes when you meet someone for the first time, you have an immediate, emotional response, and sometimes you feel an unwarranted intimacy with a stranger. This is what I felt as her hazel eyes fixed on mine. I couldn't shake the feeling that she and I had something important to do with each other. After paying my bill, I stopped at her table. She was midway through her salad. She looked up and smiled.

"Excuse me," I said, "but do we know each other?"

She put her fork down. "I don't know. I thought you looked familiar too, but I don't know from where."

Again I was struck with the deep-seated emotional response I had as I looked into her face. If I don't know her, I thought, I want to. I sat at her table while we tried to figure out where we had met before. We couldn't. Her name was Fiona. She pushed the two anchovy filets to the side of her plate. This triggered something in my brain.

"Pepperoni, black olive, and green peppers," I said.

Her eyes grew wide. "My favorite pizza."

"I knew that." I felt a chill travel up my spine.

"Are you psychic?" she asked.

"Not that I know of."

As she took another piece of lettuce into her mouth, I had a vivid image of those lips approaching mine, and for the first time in my life, I felt sexual desire for a woman. Fiona and I spent a couple of hours in conversation. Later we went for a walk through Central Park. We sat on a bench and talked some more. I went with her to her apartment. At six-thirty that evening we kissed. It felt more than familiar to kiss her. It felt like something I'd been doing for decades.

We made love. As I touched her body, I kept seeing images in my mind of loving her, as though from the past. I could almost believe that Fiona and I have been lovers before, somehow, sometime. I fell so easily into this relationship, like a resurrection.

For all I know, my subconscious has known I wanted a woman all my life, and the images created there now feel like something more mystical. Maybe I've been having this dream for years. Whatever the explanation, meeting and falling in love with Fiona was like coming home to me. I've never felt such a sense of belonging. If there is such a thing as destiny, I think this must be an example.

Kim's Story

She wore black leather head to toe, all six feet of her, and I couldn't catch my breath.

For me, it started with becoming a witch. In 1987, I read *The Mists of Avalon*, which piqued my interest in the history and practice of religions honoring the Mother Goddess. In 1991, I decided that reading wasn't enough, and I needed to meet people involved. I signed up for a course in the Old Religion at a metaphysical bookstore, and by the end of the first class, I knew I'd found what I was looking for. A practice that respected women, sexuality, the planet, and intuitive knowledge began to fill the holes in my life.

I'd broken off my last going-nowhere relationship with a man in early 1989, had had maybe two dates and no sex since. I was closed off, the sexual side of my nature was shut down and I didn't expect it to awaken again. After the class, I joined a coven, headed by Dave, a man with ten years experience with the Craft. The students were six women, four lesbians and two straight women (one of the latter being me). I didn't understand why, since the ratio of straight to gay people in general society was so much higher, things were so "off" here, but I got along with everyone, so I didn't let it bother me.

When our Labor Day weekend camping trip came, we'd been together about two and half months. The weekend was wonderful. We walked in the woods at midnight, did rituals, and made magic. On our last day I took my clothes off and showered under a tree in front of everyone. Not bad for someone who three months earlier had said that she didn't think she could ever go skyclad (the standard way to practice magic, wearing only jewelry and the ritual knife).

About a week later another barrier fell—my sex drive came back. I was painting my bathroom at the time, not generally an erotic activity. My hormones were up and running again with no outlet. It wasn't long before I met Elsa. One of the other students had bought a house that needed a lot of work, so a number of friends came over to help sand the floors. When Elsa drove her Honda up onto the lawn and let her big yellow dog out of the back seat, I sensed something interesting was about to happen.

Elsa was butch and very cute, with a wonderful personality. She's a Cancer and I'm a Scorpio, so we got along immediately. She told me later that she was flirting like mad with me, but I just thought she was being friendly. She was flirting because she just knew I was a lesbian—I had duct tape and liked power tools.

The next time I saw Elsa was Halloween, 1991, actually a Halloween party given by a witch in another coven. Halloween itself (or Samhain) is reserved for a serious ritual. Witches at a Halloween party are a lot of fun anyway, but I was particularly struck by Elsa's costume. She wore black leather, head to toe, all six feet of her, and I couldn't catch my breath. At the time, the only thought I had was, "I wish she were a man."

Elsa had been dating Sue since September, and in late December, they broke up. In the new year, I got laid off my job and went back to school. I was having a hard time making ends meet, but winter is especially difficult for me, and February is the worst. I was married in February of 1976, divorced in February of 1979, and of course there's that incredibly irritating holiday, Valentine's Day. I hate being reminded of my single status by every damned red heart in every store window.

I decided it was time to do a banishing ritual to get rid of all this old emotional baggage and make room for something new to come into my life. Did it ever. The last weekend in February was spent with Elsa, her chain saw, and several other coven members cutting down a large diseased Dutch elm in my backyard. After everyone else had gone home, Elsa and I talked at length. Our friendship was growing.

In early March, the coven gathered for the full moon observation. Three of us relaxed in a pile on the couch, Elsa, myself, and another woman. Hugging and cuddling is common among pagans, so the fact that Elsa's arm was around me was not unusual. What surprised me was my reaction to her casually touching my arm, hand, and chest. I was getting turned on, I liked it, and I wasn't the least bothered by that. Dave gave me a long look. I know he could tell what I was feeling. I began at last to understand what was happening to me, how hot I was for Elsa. Not long after that I told her I had a crush on her and thought her unbearably cute. She told me she liked me too, but had kept quiet because she thought I was straight.

Although I knew that Elsa was still not over her breakup with Sue, and wasn't available emotionally, we agreed that fooling around a little might be okay. After all, it was spring. Elsa would conduct the coven's equinox ritual, to be held in my backyard early on a Sunday morning. Saturday night we all attended a larger gathering to observe the equinox. To save driving and because she had to perform the ritual so early Sunday, Elsa planned to stay over at my house that night.

We talked, drank beer, listened to k. d. lang, and cuddled. Eventually we went to bed. I wasn't able to take the first step, so finally Elsa rolled on top of me and kissed me—the kind of soft, slow, sensuous kiss that too few men understand. It was wonderful. We did a lot of kissing, stroking, and cuddling—not much sleeping. We got through the ritual the next morning without mishap. Afterward, everyone wanted to go to breakfast, but I said I was too tired and Elsa said she wasn't ready for food. Back to bed we went for more serious making out and a little sleep.

Five days later Elsa slept over again. She stayed eighteen hours, and we spent most of it in bed. I discovered that sex with a woman is incredible. No man has ever handled me that carefully or that expertly. Maybe I was just lucky in having such a wonderful first experience. Probably not all women are like that.

Elsa and I continued our affair for three months until an easily foreseen breakup. We remain friends, and I hope this never changes because she has a very special place in my life. After four long years of nothing, she helped me become sexual again and showed me how intimacy with someone of my own sex can be far more intimate than it was with men.

Men, I believe, are basically alien beings. My marriage was a disaster that never should have happened. I do feel that if I'd learned sooner about loving my own sex, I'd have become a happier person much earlier in life. I'm happy now, though, and I believe that things happen when they're ready to happen, so there's little point in regretting the past. I hope my future includes a woman companion.

By the way, the other "straight" woman in our coven is now dating women too.

7

Lesbian in our Midst

It was sort of like when you're pregnant and suddenly you start seeing pregnant women and babies everywhere you look. Once I became aware of lesbians, I started seeing them everywhere.

I knew she was a lesbian, but I wanted to be friends anyway. See how open-minded, how politically correct, I am, I thought . . . until we kissed.

Once I knew she was a lesbian, I couldn't help staring, fascinated by this new species. Like an anthropologist, I wanted to know her culture, religious rituals, eating habits, an especially mating habits.

I told her I didn't understand lesbian sex. It must be sort of unfulfilling. So what do you do, exactly, I asked her.

✳   ✳   ✳

The women whose stories appear here were unaware of any lesbian tendencies until they discovered that they knew, and usually were friends with, a lesbian. For some reason, being aware of another woman's lesbianism worked an influence on their conscious thought. One is left with the speculation that if these women had never known a lesbian, they may never have come out.

The difference between these stories and those in the chapter I'VE BEEN VAMPED is that the lesbian acquaintances here didn't actively seduce their "straight" friends. They accepted their heterosexuality and went about their business. The seduction, then, was usually done by the story's heroine, who must have allowed herself a thought similar to, "If she's a lover of women, she could be a lover of me." That idea, perhaps frightening at first, became more and more intriguing, eventually moving them to action.

Even though the idea of their own lesbianism had never occurred to them before their association with a lesbian, most of these women were not successful heterosexuals. Many of them had never been married. They thought of themselves as independent, strong-willed, assertive, but not homosexual. However, after their first lesbian affair, they generally recognized an earlier tendency towards lesbianism.

Nadine's Story

Yes, I was trying to seduce her. I wouldn't let her do anything, of course, but I wanted her to want to.

I'm a control freak. That's what my therapy group tells me. I'm a power monger and manipulator. Yvonne would probably agree. We were coworkers and she was a lesbian. I was forty-three and married. That was three years ago. Our friendship began quite naturally, but as it grew, my subconscious need to manipulate went into high gear. As soon as I knew she needed me, I wanted to be needed more and more.

Yvonne had broken up with her lover of two years. She was unhappy and vulnerable. I preyed on her. At first all I wanted was to be essential to her. To test how far along we were, I sometimes acted aloof. I could tell the extent of her involvement by how she responded.

We talked about everything together. I found her a compassionate and loyal friend. That should have been enough. Yvonne had put a great deal of trust in me, revealing her sexual orientation. To me she talked freely about her ex-lover, and I felt privileged to be the only one she could confide in. Remembering my behavior, I can say now that it was highly flirtatious. The smiles I gave her, the affectionate touches, the intimate looks, were all designed to corral her emotions. In some corner of my brain I wanted Yvonne to fall in love with me, but I didn't understand that at the time.

When she came to work one Monday with the news that she'd been on a date, I felt violently threatened. If she found someone new, she wouldn't need me as much. That's how I thought. The next weekend she had another date, then happily came to work to tell me about it.

"She's really interesting," Yvonne told me. "She's a physical therapist."

"What happened?" I asked, consumed with curiosity.

Yvonne smiled. "We ate, we talked."

"Anything else?"

Yvonne blushed. "Kissed." She sighed.

"Is that it?"

"Yes. Besides, Nadine, there are a few things I just might not tell you."

She's already pulling away from me, I thought, panicking.

Sometimes on Thursday nights, Yvonne and I went to dinner. It was my husband's bowling night. This Thursday I invited her to my house. Yvonne brought a bottle of wine. I served a quiche and green salad. After dinner, we moved to the sofa in the living room. I had worn a low-cut blouse which displayed a little cleavage. Yes, I was trying to seduce her. I wouldn't let her do anything, of course, but I wanted her to want to.

She'd had three glasses of wine. That and the cleavage ought to do something, I reasoned. I mean, I was horny myself. She was talking about genetic research in breast cancer treatment, way above my head, but the way she looked at me, I was sure she was interested. Still, she made no move. Time was getting short, I noticed. I put my hand to her cheek, saying, "Vonnie, you're so smart. I don't understand a word of it."

I caressed her cheek. She clutched my hand in hers, then kissed the palm, lightly. Is this passion or gallantry, I wondered.

Then she moved closer to me. I turned my head away so she wouldn't kiss me. She kissed my neck. Her face was soft, not scratchy, as it glided over my skin. This is nice, I thought. She tried again to kiss my mouth, but I veered away. She kissed my collarbone, then moved to the breasts. Oh, I thought, leaning my head on the back of the sofa, this is nice. When her hand touched my breast through the cloth, I roused myself.

"No," I said, "stop."

She did.

I knew I was playing a dangerous game, but it was exciting. Yvonne came over every Thursday night after that. After dinner we'd sit together in the living room and I'd let her kiss me, eventually on the mouth as well. Kissing Yvonne was extremely erotic. She saw less of the other woman. She told me she loved me. She pushed me for sex. After a few months, she became angry, complaining that she needed more. I let her remove my blouse. The way she worked my breasts, I actually had an orgasm. I was beginning to want her to make love to me. She was so passionate and sexy, so attentive. She had told me of sex marathons involving multiple orgasms by the dozen between herself and her partners. I was beginning to believe it.

But I was married, and a heterosexual. And there was the problem of my husband coming home at ten o' clock. At nine-thirty, Yvonne had to leave. She invited me to come with her to a weekend whale-watching festival in Mendocino.

"No, I can't possibly go," I told her.

She pleaded with me. I was tempted. I turned her down. She was more than disappointed. The following Thursday, she didn't come over. Friday she wasn't at work. I called her at home and asked her to go shopping with me.

"Sorry," she said, "I'm busy." And so it was over. She couldn't take it, she said, and I couldn't take it further.

I sorely missed our Thursday evenings, and kept missing them for a long time. At work, we were civil with one another, but Yvonne kept her distance. I began to despise my husband's lovemaking. I dreamt of Yvonne's kisses. I left my husband a year later. We couldn't seem to get along at all anymore, and when there was no more sex between us, things got worse. When I confided to my therapist that I still fantasized frequently about Yvonne, she suggested I might talk to Yvonne, honestly, and try to explain it all to her.

When I understood it better myself, I did that. I told Yvonne that I'd wanted her all along, but couldn't admit that to myself, so I'd invented a manipulative game to keep her around. Yvonne forgave me. I finally let her into my pants. What joy I feel now. How wonderful and natural it is to make love with a woman. And, although I'm getting a little old for it, the all-night sex marathons really do exist.

Donna's Story

Tish smiled. "Don't be coy, hon. You don't invite a lesbian who's hot for you to dinner at your place unless you're at least toying with the idea that she might make a move on you."

When Dr. Williams suggested a support group, I balked. The thought of a bunch of self-pitying women spilling their guts to each other didn't appeal to me. She said that the psychological trauma of my breast cancer was a bigger scar than the devastation that was now my chest. Five years after a mastectomy and a divorce, she pronounced me physically fit.

I don't know exactly why my marriage failed. It could have been the scare of cancer that drove Ted away. It could have been the horror of what it had done to my body. It could have been me. Sex between us was extremely awkward after the surgery. He had always been attentive to my breasts. They had played an important role in sex. Now one of them was gone.

After I joined the support group, reluctantly, I began to understand how I had forced Ted to reject me, physically, out of shame or fear. I wasn't the only woman who had felt this way.

The group consisted of about eight women, led by Letitia Freeman, an attractive woman in her early fifties with long straight gray hair, sometimes tied at the back, and pronounced cheek bones. She wore long loose skirts and granny boots. I figured that thirty years ago she must have been a hippie. Now she was a psychologist. For several weeks I didn't participate in the confessional discussions except marginally. I listened. Mostly I listened to "Tish," as we called her. She was vibrant and blunt, expressive with her hands. She had a way of speaking that wouldn't allow you not to listen. When Tish said things like, "You're a beautiful, remarkable woman," you could believe she really meant it. She seemed to feel that way about us all. Tish hadn't had breast cancer, but her mother had died of it.

When I told my story, I guess I focused on the loss of my husband, making it seem obvious that I blamed that on the cancer.

"Maybe the loss of a breast was caused by cancer," Tish said, "but the loss of a husband? Blame yourself for that, Donna, baby."

Someone asked if I wanted him back. I said no. Someone else asked if I'd dated since. I said no.

"Decided on a life of celibacy?" Tish asked. "Boring, huh, girls?"

"Just haven't met anyone," I said.

Tish grinned. She went on to someone else. Her jewelry was silver and turquoise. You noticed the rings on her hands as she gestured. Tish didn't sit in a chair like the rest of us. She sat on a short table, rearranging her legs on it as we went along. Sometimes she took her boots off. During the week, at work, at home, I caught images of Tish floating through my conscious thoughts. She would be gesturing, wrinkling her face into frowns. Her demeanor was generally menacing. She had a way of putting psychological pressure on us; like squeezing water out of a sponge, she wrung us out.

But Tish wasn't callous, not in the least. When Carla told us one night that she had a new lump, a malignant one, Tish actually wept. And wasn't the least bit shy about doing so.

I'd been in the group almost three months when they broke me. Tish brought the subject back to my lack of interest in dating. She'd skirted the issue before, but this night she aimed at the bullseye. "You're afraid," she said. "You're ashamed. You think if you get close to someone, he won't be able to handle it. You think he might be horrified, and even show it. You're afraid of rejection."

"It's a valid fear," I argued. "The very thing happened to Marilyn." I pointed out Marilyn, although we all knew who she was.

"Yeah, it could happen. But do you really want that kind of man, Donna?"

"Even if he didn't show it, he'd be repulsed," I said. "You know what men are like about breasts. Even if he said otherwise, I'd know he was repulsed. I could tell by the way he touched the other one, or by the way he avoided that side of my body. Eventually he wouldn't want to make love to me at all. He'd

think I was a freak and he wouldn't want to be reminded." By the time I'd finished that speech, I was in tears. Tish, however, didn't intend to spare me.

"You mean, you think you're a freak. You're repulsed. Isn't that the point? You'd make sure he didn't want to touch you. You won't let anyone near you because you're ashamed. What the fuck are you ashamed of?"

A chorus of agreeing murmurs circulated the room. I didn't answer because I was crying.

"You had a disease. You had it removed. It was a mammary gland, for Christ's sake. You don't need it anymore. It was superfluous. You're beautiful, you're sexy, you're fun."

I just cried harder then, and somebody handed me a box of Kleenex.

"Okay, girls," Tish said, "it's time to go."

As they left, some of the women patted me on the back or shoulder. I couldn't stop crying. Tish and I were left alone. I blew my nose. Tish loomed over me. "Sorry, Donna," she said, her voice softer. "But you've got to get over this. You're a beautiful and remarkable woman."

"No, I'm not. You think if you say that often enough, we'll believe it. I'm not a child. I know what I look like. Nobody will ever love me again."

"Don't be ridiculous." Her voice was full of irritation. "I love you."

I shook my head, wiping my eyes. "Not like that. I meant, you know, sexual love."

"That's what I meant too." For the first time since I'd known her, I heard a slight quaver in her voice.

I looked up, shocked. Tish was looking at me tenderly. Messages shot across my brain, forming gibberish. What?" I asked. "What do you mean?"

"I'm very much attracted to you. From the first time I saw you. Something about the way you walk or talk or angle your head. I mean, maybe it doesn't mean anything to you, since I'm not a man. Men will like you just fine when you get over your insecurities about the mastectomy and become confident. You're exaggerating the reaction others will have. You're putting way too much emphasis on this. It's not you, you know? You're a complete woman."

Stuck way back on an earlier point, I said, "You love me?"

"I could, I think. I feel an attraction, a powerful one."

I was beginning to understand. "You're a lesbian?"

She laughed. "You're not very quick, are you?"

After another brief pep talk, we walked out together. Nothing more was said about Tish's feelings towards me. She didn't seem to intend to act on them. I didn't feel threatened. What I felt was flattered. She was a smart, totally together woman. What could she possibly see in me? I continued with the group, and continued to admire Tish. The smiles she aimed my way seemed more than ever affectionate. My intrigue with her deepened. Sometimes when she adjourned the meeting, I lingered and walked out to the parking lot with her. She usually went over what we'd accomplish and her own performance that night. That was how she saw it. These few minutes of conversation weren't personal. Even when she talked about me, about my progress, that is, it was in her role as counselor. I found myself wanting more, something about her, something intimate.

I'd never given much thought before to homosexuals. They were outside my sphere. And usually when I thought of them or heard about them, they were male. Curious, now that I knew a lesbian, I wanted more information. I was afraid to go to a feminist bookstore, so I picked up a copy of Nancy Friday's *Forbidden Flowers*, which I'd heard included fantasies involving women having sex with women. There were examples of these fantasies, titillating examples. I read them several times, then I tried them myself, a couple of them, the tamer ones, imagining Tish as my partner.

By the following week when group met, I had imagined poor Tish capable of extraordinary feats of lovemaking. Seeing her in person reminded me that she was a post-menopausal, ordinary woman with physical limitations. Still, I thought, it would be interesting. Like the women in the book, I could have such a fantasy and still be straight. And this beautiful and remarkable woman was interested in me. She knew about my cancer and was still interested. How could I ask her to make love to me, I wondered.

"You seem so much more confident lately," she observed after the meeting. "How do you feel?"

"Better. I think I'm really coming to terms with this."

"I'm glad." She smiled and touched my arm. "You might not need us much longer, Donna."

This thought sent me into a panic. "Oh, I still need you, Tish. I'm not weanable yet."

She took her car keys out of her macramé bag. "It's up to you."

"Tish," I said, grasping for words. "Uh, you've really been good for me, you know. I want to thank you."

"It's my job, hon. But you're welcome."

"I'd like to invite you to dinner sometime, at my place."

She looked at me silently in the artificial street light. "It's very nice of you, Donna, but unnecessary. Besides, I'm not supposed to socialize with clients."

"Well, then, maybe I could quit the group after all."

"Or former clients," she added.

"I'm not a client, Tish. You're just a group leader here. You're not even getting paid. Doesn't that make a big difference?"

She shrugged, then narrowed her eyes. I could tell she was trying to read my ulterior motive. "I suppose lack of pay goes a long way, but it's not just about money. It's also about power."

"Well, hell, I'm just asking you to dinner." I tried to laugh.

"Are you?" she asked softly. "You see, Donna, this sort of thing is always more complicated than it looks. How about having a drink with me across the street? That's harmless and I'll explain."

We ordered screwdrivers and sat at a table in a dark corner. "I shouldn't have told you about my attraction to you," she said. "Even that was manipulative. At the time I was supporting my argument that someone can love you. I didn't really think about what might result from that admission."

"Wasn't it true?"

"Oh, yes, it was true. But it's been working on your mind. You're seeing me differently now. One of the things you're seeing is my understanding and acceptance of your, in your view, flaw. That's what we're doing here, after all. You probably still feel that you'll never find someone, a man, that is, who can love you this way. In other words, you're vulnerable to my attraction to you because of the cancer, not for the right reasons."

"I just invited you to dinner," I protested.

Tish smiled. "Don't be coy, hon. You don't invite a lesbian who's hot for you to dinner at your place unless you're at least toying with the idea that she might make a move on you."

She never beat around the bush, did she? "Would you make a move on me?" I asked.

"I might." The look she gave me over the edge of her glass sent a message straight down through my stomach and out onto my vulva.

"So," she said, "you understand the predicament?"

I shook my head. "No. I'm not as vulnerable as you think. A man at work has been pursuing me for a month. He's sort of good looking and unmarried. And he knows about the mastectomy."

Tish raised an eyebrow. "Not interested?"

"No. There's nothing really wrong with him, but he's not smart enough for me. I like intelligent men. So, you see, I'm not that vulnerable. Otherwise I'd fall in his lap. I like you, Tish. I admire and respect you. Not because I'm a basket case, but because you deserve it. You're a beautiful and remarkable woman."

She laughed at my use of her words. "Very clever, hon."

Tish resisted in a noble assertion of will. A month later she asked me to conduct a workshop at the annual cancer awareness clinic which she helped organize. She wanted me to tell my story and explain the physical and psychological effects of mastectomy. I was to be co-leader with a woman who had had a lumpectomy. Tish said I was ready for such an experience, though I hesitated. Somehow I figured this was a test. She could have gotten someone else, easily. I wanted to pass her test, but didn't know what passing entailed. At the least, I thought, consenting was required. So I did it.

One of the requirements was to show a photograph of my chest. This was the hardest part. Even having the photo taken was horrible. But I kept thinking of Tish and how she wanted me to be. I went through the ordeal without too much suffering. I found it far easier to talk about my cancer after having been in the support group, and the women there were understanding and interested. And afraid. They asked questions and we answered very personally. One woman said that her lover had just discovered a malignant tumor. How courageous, I thought, to say that among strangers. The experience was actually a high. The spirit of the gathering was celebratory and compassionate. This is what I reported to Tish over the phone the next day. She had been there, she told me. She'd been spying on me.

"I'm very proud of you," she said. "You don't need to come to group anymore, hon."

But I wanted to come. It was the only time I could see her. That two hours had become the high point of my week. I was devastated to think I'd be cut off from her inspiration.

"So find something better to do with your Wednesday nights," she told me. "As for Friday, how about dinner at your place?"

Louise's Story

I seduced her, frankly.

Although I'd played the straight game all my adult life without finding a permanent mate, at forty-three, I didn't think anything was wrong. I just thought I was unsuccessful at attracting men. If I was myself with them, that is, strong, self-reliant, assertive, they ran like rabbits, and I wasn't able to give up being those things. So I remained single.

I knew Anne for three years before she came out to me, and seven more before we became lovers. She never made a move toward me, other than to say she loved me as a friend. She was remarkably loyal for ten years, during which we both continued to have affairs with other people.

Then Anne lost her job. I was living alone, so I asked her to share my home with me until she got back on her feet. Shortly after she moved in, I felt the need for more than friendship. She was pretty vulnerable at that point, as well as unattached. I seduced her, frankly.

It was a revelation. Everything clicked. I knew I had found my mate. We've been together ever since, seven years, and it is indeed a lifetime commitment. Anne is more religious than I am, though I too believe in God. Our strong faith and moral values have kept us together and made us work hard on our relationship when times were tough, such as when I had to go to war or other locations required by duty.

I'm retiring from the military in a couple of months, thank God. Then, perhaps, I'll be able to be more active in the gay rights movement.

Tracy's Story

Where does one draw the line, I asked myself, between sexual and non-sexual love? I enjoyed her company. I missed her when she was away. I felt happy and secure with her hand in mine. I felt total trust.

I'd always loved my career as a pilot, and blamed my bachelor life on that. I dated lots of men, lived with one for six months, but never found one I wanted to marry. After an ugly breakup when I was thirty-eight, I gave up dating altogether. There didn't seem to be any point in it, other than sex, of course. Eventually you get used not to having that, though, so at forty-five, I was content, successful, and rarely lonely. My network of friends spanned the globe. Whenever I felt the need for human companionship, I looked one of them up.

My oldest friend lived in Boulder, Colorado. Janie and I met in college and had managed to keep up with one another, though visits were sometimes several years apart. She lived with her teenage son in the house she'd raised her children in. Four years ago she divorced her husband, got a real estate license, and started a new life.

In 1997, I got badly injured in an automobile accident. I was grounded. During the early part of my rehabilitation to regain the use of my legs and left hand, I stayed with my sister and her husband in Akron, Ohio. This was a terrible time in my life. I felt useless, hopeless, and frustrated. Along with the tedious rehabilitative exercises, I was treated for depression. This was the only time I'd ever regretted my independent lifestyle. I used to sit in that wheelchair and ask myself why I hadn't married my high school sweetheart and had four children. By now, they'd be adults and could take care of me.

With one good arm, I could at least write. I wrote to everyone I knew, including Janie, who called as soon as she got the letter. She offered to come visit me, but I was feeling so worthless that I told her to stay away.

Despite my moodiness, I had a stubborn will to succeed and made steady progress. My sister and brother-in-law were wonderful, but this was a terrible strain on them. By the time I could walk, jerkily, we were all ready for me to move out. Janie and I had been talking on the phone all these months, and more than once, she'd invited me to come stay with her, citing my misfortune as the only chance we'd ever had of an extended visit. When I felt adequately unburdenlike, I accepted her invitation and moved to Boulder and Janie's guest room. The arrangement was perfect. Charlie, Janie's son, was in his last year of high school and working part time. He wasn't home much, but when he was, we got along well. I became a sort of "wife" for Janie, cooking, doing her laundry, taking care of all the domestic chores. We were ideally suited as housemates, and our friendship finally got a chance to flourish. We'd stay up late at night talking and giggling. On weekends, we'd often go for drives, and sometimes we went fishing. Meanwhile, my physical condition improved. I prayed for the day I'd get my wings back.

There was no man in Janie's life. She said she didn't want one, and since I'd felt much the same, I didn't question it. Even the fact that she had a few lesbian friends didn't make me suspicious, not at first. Lots of them around these days, after all. After I'd been there about three months, Janie told me she was a lesbian. That's why she got divorced, over a woman. We talked a lot about Janie's love life after that, about the two other women she'd slept with. I found out that while I'd been living in her house, she'd been seeing someone. A real estate agent doesn't keep any kind of regular schedule, so it was easy enough for her to hide it. But she didn't want to hide it from me. And Charlie already knew. The woman she'd been seeing was on the wane, she said. It just wasn't working out.

After the initial shock, I didn't find any of this disturbing. It was sort of interesting, actually. I was curious about how Janie could have been a lesbian and not known it until her forties. She said that she always had been one. She knew that now, looking back. It seemed unbelievable to me. Life is full of ironies, isn't it? I made her promise to tell her lesbian friends that we weren't lovers. I didn't want them to get the wrong idea about me. Things went on as before between us. Janie vaguely searched for a new lover.

Janie and I had always been very physical with one another, hugging and touching freely. I noticed that the touching gradually became more intimate. We often sat together on the sofa, holding hands in front of the television. Janie would kiss me goodnight now on the cheek or forehead. I wasn't afraid of this closeness. It felt quite natural. Being with Janie gave me a sense of comfort, a warmth I'd never known before. The emotional bond between us was deep and honest. This physical expression of it seemed almost obligatory.

One morning Charlie asked me if I was in love with his mother. "Of course not," I told him. "We're just good friends. You know I'm straight."

Charlie's question prompted me to reexamine my relationship with Janie. Where does one draw the line, I asked myself, between sexual and nonsexual love? I enjoyed her company. I missed her when she was away. I felt happy and secure with her hand in mine. I felt total trust. How would it be different if we slept together? I couldn't answer my question. Whenever Janie described to me what she was looking for in a mate, she described something identical to what we had. Except for sex. Celibate marriages are not unheard of. Maybe they were like this. Sex just gets in the way, anyway, I told myself. That's why my friendship with Janie would last forever. It wouldn't be destroyed by sex.

One night she came home to tell me she had a date. She'd met a woman, a new client. She was beautiful, she was intelligent, she was a lesbian. I was consumed with jealousy and shocked at my response. I rationalized it, citing the very real threat of my being ousted if Janie found someone.

The night of her date, I waited up for her, crazy. By midnight, I was sure that she wasn't coming home, that she was in bed with her new love. When she did come home, about one in the morning, she found me in the family room, sobbing. Janie sat beside me and held me, asking me what was wrong. I regained my composure, assured her there was nothing wrong, and asked how the date went.

"Okay," she said. "We had a lovely dinner, then went for drinks. We talked."

"That's it?"

She nodded.

"Did you like her?"

"Yes."

"Will you see her again?"

"Haven't decided. And she'll have something to say about that, too." Janie stroked my cheek, then kissed it. "Tell me what you were crying about, Trace."

I love it when she touches me like this, I thought. We sat in the semi-darkness, close, our hands clasped together. I could smell the subtle rose-petal aroma of her perfume. At that moment I knew I'd been lying to myself. This wasn't a platonic friendship. Maybe it never had been. I kissed Janie on the mouth and told her I loved her. We slept in the same bed that night, holding each other.

The following day we became lovers. I hesitate to say it that way, since in a sense, we were already lovers. Sex did make a difference, though, more than I thought it would. Before Janie, sex had been fun, physical pleasure. But now it was so much more. It was a beautiful, intimate sharing, a truly spiritual experience. Like Janie, I suppose I've been a lesbian all my life.

I'm almost fully recovered from the accident, looking forward to returning to work. But things will be different from now on. I'm going to get a regular route, a job that will allow me to come home at night. Charlie will soon be moving out on his own. Janie says she can sell houses anywhere, so she can follow me to my new post. After a lifetime of wandering the globe, I now have a home and a center for my life. I don't believe in God, but could almost believe that there was something providential about the accident that led me to Janie.

8

Like a Virgin

I guess I'm still afraid to have sex with a woman, even though I really want to do it.

My last boyfriend called me a dyke whenever he wanted sex and I didn't. I guess he was right. He was my "last" boyfriend.

I was forty-five before I started looking for a woman. Now I'm looking for her with a driving need. I want to get laid by a lesbian before my forty-sixth birthday.

*   *   *

In this chapter, I've included stories from women who have recently come out and haven't yet had a lesbian affair. Most of them are actively searching for a lover. Some of them aren't quite sure how to go about it. Maybe this book can help, giving as it does several examples of successful seduction.

Margaret's Story

I hope someday I can find a close loving friend, but at this point, it's enough for me to be brave enough to be "out."

I began to suspect I was a lesbian in 1987 when I joined the Sweet Adelines, a women's barbershop singing group. I'd been going with men since I was fourteen, but was always very unhappy. I kept trying, though, because I wanted to be like everybody else.

When I was fourteen, I started a secret relationship with a priest. After about six months, I wanted to stop it, but I was afraid and didn't know how to break it off. After I went to college at eighteen, I finally got the courage to break it off.

Up to the age of twenty-seven, I had a number of relationships with men that were short-lived and unhappy. Being with men made me very depressed. At twenty-seven, I decided I was tired of being alone and moved in with a man who was twenty-five years older than me. I never really liked him but I thought I could get used to being with him. He was verbally abusive towards me and I was extremely unhappy. It took me nearly seven years to get the courage to leave.

On May 17, 1988, there was a house fire and I decided that day that I was getting out of this terrible relationship.

In 1995, I had developed a love for a woman in the Sweet Adelines. I didn't tell her because she was a staunch Catholic and I was sure she would be very displeased. Eventually, the infatuation faded. We're still good friends.

As far as romance goes, I am alone and isolated. A few months ago I started subscribing to a gay magazine. I really look forward to each issue. When I read it, I can feel a connection with other people like me.

I hope someday I can find a close loving friend, but at this point, it's enough for me to be brave enough to be "out." My life is still far from perfect, but as a result of my awakening, I have ended the destructive relationships with men and developed some important platonic relationships with women. At age forty, I've finally started to take steps to accept what I am.

May's Story

The more I learned and the more I associated with lesbians, the more I began to reassess myself.

I've only recently made the decision to go for it. I'm forty-four and twice divorced. The first marriage was a disaster, and the second, although amicable, was short-lived and disappointing, for both of us. But my failed marriages and general dissatisfaction with men alone didn't bring me to this point. It was primarily my niece Jill.

Jill and I always shared a special relationship, from the day she was born. I didn't have any children of my own, and Jill was the first of my sister's. When Jill was twenty-five, three years ago, she told me she was a lesbian. She told her mother about the same time, as she'd made an agonizing decision to "come out to us" after too many years of deception. We were all surprised, as Jill had all along pretended to be dating and enjoying the company of men. In reality, she had been enjoying the company of women since she was eighteen. It was her commitment to her lover at the time (and still) that prompted her to come out.

I was uncomfortable at first, but my sister was totally unreasonable. Patty said she would still treat Jill as her daughter, would always love her, but she forbade Jill's lover entry into her house, and she forbade Jill from mentioning her. Jill went through a rough time dealing with her mother's rejection of her lifestyle. I felt I had to compensate for it, I guess, by being extra understanding. Jill and I and her lover Connie had lots of serious talks. I had lots of talks with Patty. I began to get an education about homosexuality.

Eventually, I joined our local PFLAG chapter and talked to other people with gay children and friends. Patty refused to join. The more I learned and the more I associated with lesbians, the more I began to reassess myself. I had never been really attracted to men, and had never felt honest with them. I had had some very special friendships with women, emotionally intense ones, and I'd even had some physical desire for women from time to time, but had never let it develop into anything.

I gradually came to feel a kinship with the lesbians I met through Jill and through PFLAG. I met some who, like me, had become lesbians in their forties. Their stories sounded very familiar. When I first "confessed" to Jill that I thought I might be a lesbian, she became distraught. She blamed herself. I told her that if she were responsible for my enlightenment, it was a priceless gift, the gift of self knowledge, the gift of truth, and I was grateful to her.

I've never been a very happy person. Now I think perhaps it's because I've never known who I was, have never known how to go about satisfying my desires.

Poor Patty—her only daughter and her only sister. I have some hope that the added pressure of my new identity will finally persuade her to try to be understanding. She can't afford to abandon everybody. I've seen some progress already. Patty has now met Connie, and I know from seeing it happen over and over that it's much harder to hate in the particular than it is in general. Jill has gotten over her guilt about me, and she and Connie are now taking an avid interest in my indoctrination. They're trying to get me to adopt a cat because they know this gorgeous veterinarian who's just perfect for me.

I can hardly wait.

Valerie's Story

When someone gives you hope in a dark time of life, it's natural to crave union, to want to connect physically and emotionally.

When I was forty-two, a year and a half after divorcing my husband of twelve years, I had the luck to fall in love with an astonishingly wonderful woman. We are not acquainted, nor ever likely to be, but she has opened up wellsprings in me that I never knew were there. She's an artist of exceedingly rare beauty and she possesses a spiritual clarity, a soul truth, to which we all aspire.

When someone gives you hope in a dark time of life, it's natural to crave union, to want to connect physically and emotionally. The desire is real, even though there's no opportunity to act on it. Love makes us grow anyhow. I'm a better person for having had this opening, spiritually, politically, and artistically.

Sarah's Story

I'll be sixty on my next birthday, a grandmother who lived a normal life, a lesbian who has never made love to a woman.

When I was sixteen I fell in love with my best friend Kate. We thought we were practicing for boys, learning how to kiss, learning what it would feel like to have our breasts fondled. Kate's older sister caught us. Our parents were horrified and forbade us to see each other again. We tried to disobey, but they were vigilant. I ached all over for Kate, but I never got to be in her arms again.

For many months I was admonished about how perverted and wicked homosexuals were, how that was the last thing I'd ever want to be. I believed it. I prayed to God to make me normal.

I married at nineteen, a man I wasn't in love with. Sex with him was pleasant at first, but there was no passion between us. I thought of Kate often. My husband died two years ago. We had two children, grown women now with children of their own. A few years ago I became friends with a lesbian. I envied her, I feared her. As we became closer and I recognized my own developing desires towards her, I stupidly destroyed our friendship.

I can no longer suppress my sexuality. I'll be sixty on my next birthday, a grandmother who lived a normal life, a lesbian who has never made love to a woman. The shame I was made to feel at sixteen has been sufficient to keep me in line all these years. I still think of Kate often. I miss her still.

Appendix
THE SURVEY

The survey which follows was the source of all statistics and conclusions drawn in this book. In addition to these questions, participants were asked to write an optional narrative about their awakening to lesbianism. The results formed the preceding content.

Survey Number _____
LATE BLOOMERS SURVEY

Please answer the following questions as accurately as possible. If a question does not apply to your situation or you prefer not to answer, skip it. The ? choice for some of the questions should be circled if you don't know or are unsure.

1. What is your age? _____

2. What is your profession? _____

3. What is your educational background?
   _____ Less than high school graduation
   _____ High school graduation
   _____ Some college
   _____ A.A. degree
   _____ Bachelor's degree

_____ Master's degree

_____ Doctorate

4. At what age did you have your first sexual encounter with a woman (if ever)? _____

5. At what age did you first identify yourself as a lesbian (if ever)?

_____

6. At what age did you first have intercourse with a man (if ever)?

_____

7. Have you had any male lovers since learning of your lesbian tendencies? Y N

8. Circle the term which best describes your view of your sexuality now:

    Homosexual Bisexual Heterosexual

9. What is your legal marital status:

    Married Separated Divorced Widowed Single, never married

10. If you've been married, please answer the following:

How many years did your marriage(s) last?

_____ _____ _____

11. How many female lovers have you had? _____

12. Of the 5 or fewer most significant lesbian relationships you've had, what were the ages of yourself and your lover when they began? Also, record the number of years the relationship(s) lasted. If you are still

with one of these women, put a plus sign + after the number of years.

Your Age   Her Age   Years Together

_____   _____   ____

_____   _____   ____

_____   _____   ____

_____   _____   ____

_____   _____   ____

13. In general, have you remained friends with female ex-lovers?
    Y N

14. In general, have you remained friends with male ex-lovers?
    Y N

15. How many children do you have? _____

16. Are you out with friends? Y N
    with family? Y N
    in business? Y N

17. If you are not living as an openly gay person, even with friends and family, what is the primary reason for your not coming out?
    _____ Fear of persecution
    _____ Fear of loss of business/loss of job
    _____ Fear of loss of status
    _____ Fear of loss of friends and family
    _____ Lack of identification with homosexuals
    _____ Guilt
    _____ Other_____

18. Are your parents/siblings accepting and supportive of your lesbianism? Y N ?

19. Are you pro-choice?   Y N ?

20. Are you a member of any women's organization? Y N

21. Are you a member of any gay organization?   Y N

22. Do you consider yourself a gay rights activist? Y N

23. Do you consider yourself a women's rights activist?   Y N

24. Are any of your siblings gay? Y N ?

25. Are either of your parents gay? Y N ?

26. Do you believe that your attraction to women is innate, perhaps genetic? Y N ?

27. Do you believe that loving women is a choice that you have made? Y N ?

28. Have you had professional counseling directly related to your sexual identity? Y N

29. Do you consider your heterosexual early life an attempt to delude yourself? Y N ?

30. Do you believe that you could someday be a happy member of a heterosexual couple? Y N ?

31. Are you happier as a lesbian than you were before you knew? Y N ?

32. Was there anything about your childhood behavior to suggest homosexual tendencies (excessive tomboyishness, unusual crushes on girls)? Y N ?

33. Did you seek out your first female lover? Y N ?

34. Did your first sexual encounter with a woman come out of a close friendship? Y N

35. If so, was she a lesbian? Y N ?

36. Were you the first female lover of your first female lover?   Y N

37. If you are currently in a relationship, do you live with your lover? Y N

38. Do you consider yourself religious? Y N ?

39. If so, what denomination? _____

About the Author

Robin McCoy is a writer and computer professional living in a happily committed relationship in Central California. She has published articles in numerous national magazines and has won awards for her fiction.

Made in the USA
Lexington, KY
04 August 2011